HOPE

WHEN THE NIGHT DOESN'T END

ROBERTO MORALES

"LIFE IS A JOURNEY…

and you are the Commander of your expedition."

The author

Disclaimer:

This book is a firsthand account of real-life events, as narrated by the author to the best of his recollection. While every effort has been made to accurately depict these events, it is important to note that due to the stressful and traumatic nature of the experiences, individuals involved may remember details differently or incompletely. Additionally, to protect the privacy and anonymity of certain individuals, some names have been changed or omitted.

Book cover and formatting style designed by the author.

Dear reader,

The name "Esperanza" holds dual significance. Commonly a female name in Spanish-speaking cultures, it also serves as a powerful noun meaning "Hope." This duality imbues the word with layers of meaning, symbolizing the resilience of the human spirit and the optimistic vision that drives us forward. May this book convey the essence of 'Esperanza'—Hope in the face of unimaginable challenges.

Sincerely,

Roberto Morales

Tribute

In memory of Mr. Arturo Cobo, a cherished friend, a mentor, and an exemplary human being. A valiant Cuban-freedom fighter, he proudly served as a member of the 2506 Brigade during the Bay of Pig invasion to overthrow the Castro regime. He dedicated his life to help those who -like myself- escaped from Cuba and survived the treacherous journey across the Florida Straits.

In solemn tribute to the volunteers of the organization 'Brothers to the Rescue'—Armando Alejandre Jr., Carlos Costa, Mario de la Peña, and Pablo Morales—whose lives were tragically cut short on February 24th, 1996. They perished when their two Cessna Skymaster planes were shot down by two Cuban Air Force MiG-29s. May their courageous spirits forever inspire us.

Dedication

This book is dedicated to the relentless dreamers, those who persist in their pursuits and never give up despite the trials and passage of time. And especially to those who gave their utmost, even if the journey did not lead them to their intended destination.

With eternal gratitude to:

❖ God, for bestowing upon me the gift of a second chance.

❖ my mother, María del Carmen, whose legacy of courage and unshakable determination runs through my veins.

❖ my beloved wife, Ericka, whose unwavering support breathed life into this book.

❖ my amazing children, Alexa Marie and Robert Daniel, my greatest source of inspiration and joy.

❖ my brother, Carlos. Without him, this story would have never happened.

❖ my sister, Zady, for her help and complicity.

❖ the members of the surveillance team, friends and relatives, whose courage made our daring escape possible.

❖ Isabel Álvarez and Malaysia Otero. Their insightful feedback has greatly improved this manuscript.

Acknowledgments

With heartfelt appreciation to my editor, Ms. Gillian McDonald.

ESPERANZA
(HOPE)

Escale 1:20

Leyend
1. Farm tractor neumatic (1 x 6' diameter)
2. Autobus neumatics (4 x 4' diameter)
3. Wooden Estructure
4. Keels or Cetreboards (2)
5. Rudder
6. Oars (4)
7. Mast
8. Mainsail
9. Small Sail / Jib
10. Tensors (3): Forestay (1), Backstay (2)

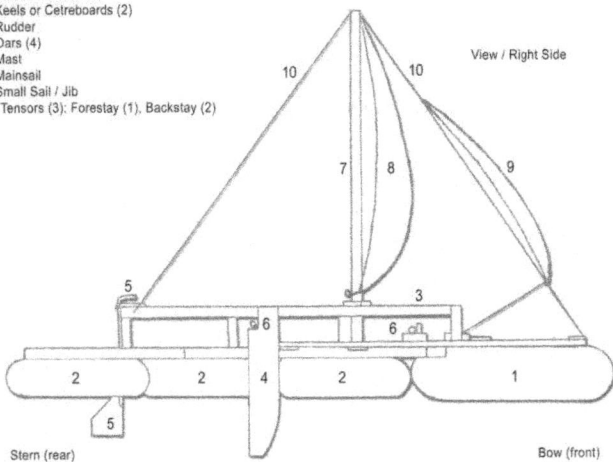

View / Right Side

Stern (rear)   Bow (front)

Designed by Roberto. *Note*: 1:20 represents the scale of the original drawing. This graphic has been reduced for editing purposes.

Contents

The Last Hour 1

The Spark 15

The Point of no Return 57

The Departure 109

The Next Day 137

The Tide 171

A New Day 191

A Hectic Night 203

The Return to Life 219

Hope I

Postscript II

Ten years later V

Tribute to the Crew VII

Beyond the Horizon: A New Life VIII

About the Author X

1

THE LAST HOUR

Monday, May 24th, 1993. Boca Ciega beach, east of Havana City, Cuba.

"Shouldn't we wait till tomorrow?" Roberto asks. A slight tremor in his voice betrays his anxiety as he examines the stormy firmament.

Fast-moving clouds flee in panic from the approaching storm brewing in the east. The howling wind has chased away the usual night sounds. Like tiny projectiles, sand grains strike anyone brave enough to face the invisible force. A scent of saltpeter fills the air. Trying to listen to the crickets chirping or wander the streets searching for nightlife are pointless. The roads are deserted, and the waves rumble, pounding against the beach like a beast mauling the entire coastline.

Roberto, 26, with dark hair and a slim frame, is not what one might expect from someone with his skills. Standing at 5'

6" feet tall and weighing about 135 pounds, he is unassuming, but his interests reveal a sharp mind with a love of sports and reading. However, he is not a traditional reader who reads for pure entertainment. Just two fiction titles have passed through his hands. His passions lie in the sciences: physics, mathematics, astronomy, philosophy, and psychology. He devours any publication offering new knowledge, always eager to seek an answer to the unexpected questions posed by his friends. His buddies call him 'The Philosopher.'

Roberto served for three years in the army as a member of a special reconnaissance team. He specialized in military intelligence, rising to the rank of platoon sergeant. He spent hundreds of drill hours infiltrating imaginary enemy lines during his training. Tonight, Roberto's skills are being put to the test.

"Bro, are you out of your mind? The longer we wait, the greater the chance of being caught," Gerardo's voice booms, cutting through the howling wind.

Gerardo is 27. His stark blond hair sets him apart, and his robust physique matches his thick, metallic voice. He's been Roberto's best friend since childhood. Being an only child, Gerardo sees Roberto as the brother he never had.

The two men are seniors at Havana's Institute of Sports and Physical Education. Both are experts in orienteering, a challenging cross-country sport requiring a sharp eye for map reading and compass navigation.

The youngsters stand facing west, the wind blowing on their backs. They shield their eyes and mouths from the flying sand from the east. Roberto raises his gaze again and watches the stormy sky, his eyes narrowed into a squint. A thin, silvery curve emerges from the tumultuous clouds, announcing the crescent moon phase has begun.

"Didn't the calendar say it's a new moon tonight?" Roberto asks, looking up.

"Yeah, that's what it says."

"Shit, you can't even trust the calendar," Roberto mutters, shaking his head.

His friend stares at him, eyebrows knitted in confusion. "What's wrong?"

Roberto gestures skyward, disbelief and disappointment in his face. "See the moon?"

"Yeah!" Gerardo tilts his head back, peering upwards.

"Exactly. There shouldn't be a moon." Roberto takes a deep breath and nods, "You're right, it's gotta be tonight. Let's get back to the group."

They had chosen this specific date because, according to the calendar, it was the start of a new moon phase, and the lack of moonlight would render the night darker. This is precisely what they needed: absolute darkness, making them almost invisible. Unfortunately, things don't always go as planned. Because of a printing error in the calendar, tonight is the start of the crescent moon phase. Hence, the upcoming nights will be clearer and more dangerous for their mission.

Both men are members of a team meeting in secrecy in a house on 440th Street, one block from the beach. The humble dwelling battles time to preserve its fading white paint. The skin coating finish is missing in some spots, exposing the red clay bricks beneath. Despite most of the metal plates being corroded by rust, the number 105 is still visible next to the entrance. At first glance, there is nothing special about this home. It would go unnoticed in the sight of passersby. However, for the people hiding inside, this house has become a silent accomplice to their covert plans.

On the porch, a distraction group of seven people provides coverage for the team inside. They chat, laugh, sip drinks, and dance to music coming from a portable cassette player, creating the illusion of a casual gathering. It is all an artificial scene, an intended distraction carefully crafted by Roberto.

Inside the house, five men work in the dark to avoid unwanted attention from their neighbors. They are assembling a small homemade raft conveniently brought inside in pieces. The 'Balsa,' as Cubans call these rafts, will be their vessel for a one-way expedition in pursuit of a dream. Thus, they called their boat Esperanza, a common female name that means hope in the islanders' tongue. They have prepared for this moment for two years, working in secret and keeping the noise down. They have taken every precaution to elude the Cuban authorities and informants.

It's past 9 o'clock when the front door opens with an abrupt whoosh, and the outside light floods the confined living room where the men labor. Carmen, Roberto's mother and a member of the surveillance group, stumbles in, her face twisted with fear and her hands shaking.

"Son, I think someone ratted us to the police," she says, her voice trembling. "There's a cop on the corner, and he's looking over here."

Carmen, small and curvy, is approaching her fifties. Her affable personality and willingness to help others have won her the love of everyone who knows her. At age 34, Carmen was suddenly widowed, leaving her with the burden of raising her three children, Carlos, Roberto, and Zady. She raised them on her own with unwavering determination, dedicating herself to their upbringing and providing them with love and care in the absence of their departed father. The government did not provide any useful welfare services to widows or single mothers.

Dumbfounded, the group exchanges bewildered glances. Their heavy breathing is the only sound in the room. A temporary paralysis takes over their bodies as two years of clandestine work hangs by a thread.

"Bro, they'll have to drag us out of here," Gerardo breaks the silence with a defiant tone, his furrowed brow drawn together and his eyes filled with rage.

"Easy, man, easy. We don't yet know what he wants," Roberto says calmly. "Let's finish tying these tubes... and we'll see what happens."

The cramped room remains obscured, preventing outsiders from seeing what is transpiring inside. On the porch, the members of the surveillance group carry on their fake celebration to mask any suspicious behavior.

"I think he is looking at the girls," Aunt Titi whispers to her sister, Carmen.

Aunt Titi is two years older than Carmen. She stands out from her sister with her messy, dyed blonde hair and tall, slim figure, yet their personalities are almost identical.

"I hope you're right," Ramon interrupts with pessimism in his voice. He places a cigarette in his mouth and digs into his shirt pocket for a lighter. As he strikes the lighter's ignition, he takes a quick glance at the cop out of the corner of his eye.

Ramon, Carmen's late husband's cousin, is in his forties and of medium height. Since his cousin's passing, Ramon has always been ready to help Carmen's family when needed. He is the sole man on the surveillance team.

"Girls, go inside and put something on. You ain't going back to the beach, are you?" Aunt Titi suggests to Zady and Diany, the two young women who are still in bathing suits, a hint of irony in her voice.

Zady, 21, is Roberto's sister. She is a senior chemical engineering student with long, raven-colored, undulating tresses. Her well-defined curves magnify the archetypal figure of the Cuban woman. Diany is also 21. She is a ravishing, slim, brown-haired woman in her last year of nursing school. She is there to support her boyfriend, Raul, a fellow member of the escape team. Both women are in the bloom of their time, and their enchanting beauty captivates any man's eye.

The two young women enter the house to change their clothes.

Meanwhile, inside the building...

Carlos strives to fasten the last inner tube to the wooden frame. Two years ago, he hatched the idea of escaping the island on a raft. Carlos is the same height as Roberto, his younger brother, but his exercise routine makes his body more muscular and toned. Baseball and spearfishing rank high among his favorite sports.

"Ready! Esperanza is ready!" Carlos exclaims.

Zady and Diany return to the porch dressed in t-shirts and shorts. Meanwhile, Roberto examines the exit door, noting the frame's right-hand surface is smoother, and the hinges are on the left side. The house's front door is slender, but it is the only exit. Thus, passing the fifteen by four feet structure through the narrow door will not be easy. Turning the raft on one side is the obvious solution.

"The tubes gotta go on the right so the hinges don't mess them up," Roberto concludes.

The five crew members strategize how to maneuver the

heavy raft out of the building. Just as they plan their next move, Carmen rushes in with the news they've all been waiting for.

"He's leaving! The cop is leaving, but you can't get out yet," she says, panting.

With the policeman gone, the crew members double-check their supplies one last time, ensuring they have everything needed to survive the treacherous journey ahead.

"We're all set... the compass, life jackets, backpacks, and Esperanza." The five men inspect their gear, making sure nothing is left behind.

"Dang, we almost forgot the diesel!" Roberto says, grabbing the bottle and shoving it in the nearest backpack.

The bottle of diesel was originally an old wine glass jar. For years, Carmen used it in her kitchen to store cooking oil. Repurposed as a diesel container, the bottle has a plug made from a rice sack to allow the fuel to leak out. Once at sea, Roberto intends to tie the bottle to the vessel's bow below the waterline. He knows sharks have a keen sense of smell, so he believes dispersing fuel in the water will keep these marine animals away.

"What about the tank with water and sugar? How are we gonna carry it?" Raul asks.

Raul is extremely thin. At 5' 10" feet tall, he weighs only 113 lbs. An eating disorder is not the cause of his anorexic look; malnutrition has taken a toll on his body. Despite only being 27 years old, his gray hair makes him look older.

"Oh! Hadn't thought of that," Carlos says.

The ten-gallon tank, filled with a mixture of water and brown sugar, is heavy. Its high carbohydrate content and extended lifespan make it the expedition's primary food source. Two men need to make an extra trip to conceal the container near the shore.

"I'll go," Raul volunteers for the task.

"Let Gonzalez go instead," Roberto suggests, trying to restrict Raul's physical activities.

Gonzalez, 26, is Raul's cousin. He has black curly hair and a sharp nose. His Arabic appearance and height distinguish him from the rest. Despite being the team's youngest member, he is the tallest and strongest, standing at six feet and weighing 180 pounds.

"He can't right now," Carlos says, gesturing toward a corner of the room where Gonzalez is on his knees, praying.

"Hey, I can do this," Raul insists with determination.

"Okay."

Roberto agrees, carefully cracking the door open and peeking outside.

"Ramon, come inside."

The man enters the room and closes the door behind him with a gentle click. Roberto describes the mission, and

Ramon's eyes widen in understanding as he nods.

"Got it! I'm ready."

"Alright, let's go," Raul's voice echoes off the walls.

They pick up the container and leave the house, heading toward the coast.

Shortly after, the men reach the beach and conceal the tank behind some dune grasses near the point of departure. With haste, they walk away from the container and pause to regain their breath. As salty ocean air fills their lungs, the sound of crashing waves rumbles in the night. After a brief rest, they rush back to the house, their breath coming in quick, heavy bursts. Upon reaching the building, Ramon remains outside on the porch, his eyes sharp and watchful, while Raul slips inside and rejoins his clandestine team.

"The tank is ready," Raul says, panting.

"Good! Get dressed, it's time," his teammates urge him.

Like his friends, Raul puts on military clothes and a hat made of palm leaves. The young crew agreed to wear military uniforms Roberto had kept from his days in the army. These uniforms would provide camouflage, helping them blend into the night's darkness. The outfits would also shield the crew from the sun's harsh rays and keep them warm during chilly nights.

The clock is ticking toward 9:30 p.m., departure time, and a palpable tension charges the air. Their hearts pound inside their chests, and their breath comes in quick, shallow intakes. Sweat trickles down their foreheads, glistening in the scarce light.

"Let's roll her onto her side," Roberto says, his voice barely above a whisper, yet his command reverberates like a thunderclap through the crew's ears.

The men strap on their backpacks and swarm around Esperanza. Loaded with four oars, a mast with two sails, a rudder, six vehicle inner tubes, and provisions, the raft weighs over 300 pounds. Grunting with effort, the crew lift the boat off the ground and turn it sideways. They hurry with the heavy load toward the door leading to the street, ready to embark on their journey.

"We're screwed!" Ramon says, bursting into the room, followed by Carmen. Their pale faces speak to the gravity of the situation. "Four guards are coming... and they're armed! Someone ratted us out."

A chill runs through the room following Ramon's words, and a deafening silence takes over. The wind's whistle fades away. In the minds of the five young men, the image of a hopeful tomorrow turns into dark shades of prison bars. If they get caught, they'll face the consequences of living in total social segregation for the rest of their lives.

"Sneak out and see what they want," Raul whispers to Ramon.

Ramon takes a deep breath and wipes away the beads of

sweat from his face. Calming himself, he heads back to the porch, accompanied by Carmen, who closes the door behind her. Meanwhile, inside the house, the five young men remain motionless, silent, holding their breath. Their hearts race, pounding within their chests.

The patrol, comprising four soldiers armed with automatic AK-47 rifles, advances toward the house. Anxiety and fear increase among the support team as the guards approach. Their faces are pale, and cold sweat trickles down their temples. When they reach the gate separating the porch from the street, one soldier steps forward and addresses the group.

"Good evening, comrades!"

"Good evening!" Ramon replies coolly, though his body is screaming with tension.

"Have a light? I need to light my cigarette," the soldier asks.

"Yes, yes! Of course!" Ramon answers, the corners of his mouth pulling up into an artificial grin. As he reaches for the disposable lighter in his shirt pocket, the sound of his breathing is muffled in the silence. He nervously extends both hands toward the guard's face. His hands shake as he flicks the lighter. The spark fizzles and quickly dies out, leaving no trace of a flame. Ramon's thumb reddens from the effort as it repeatedly strikes the knurled thumbwheel, but the ignition still refuses to start.

"Just work, you son of a..."

In frustration, Ramon's thoughts curse the dirt-cheap lighter. Having to go to the kitchen for matches means opening the front door and exposing what hides behind it: the raft and its crew.

Finally, a tiny flame appears.

The wind howls as it beats down on the weak, yellowish fire. Ramon's left hand trembles as he cups it to cover the meager blaze. The soldier, cigarette dangling from his lips, leans in toward the warmth of the fire.

These terrifying seconds seem to stretch on for an eternity, as if life itself has stopped.

And behind the door, the five young men's thoughts travel back in time as memories of their pasts come alive.

The rented house, hours before departure. From left to right: Mr. Perez, Gerardo, Estela, Aunt Titi, Yeney, Carlos, Gonzalez, Carmen, Raul, Roberto, and Zady. Photo taken by Ramon.

Main Ave and 440 Street intersection (view from the sand). The rented house (not visible in this picture) is behind the two-story building on the left.

2

THE SPARK

The summer of 1991 dawned, enveloping the Caribbean in record-breaking temperatures. It felt distinct, with an aura of heat, restlessness, and suffocation. People wandered the city streets, their faces somber and devoid of joy with a dull look in their eyes. Hunger and desperation had eroded their civility, turning them into mere survivors. Even a glimpse of a bag hinting at food was enough to entice predatory stares. Hunger erased good manners.

After the collapse of the Soviet Union and the fall of communist regimes in Eastern Europe, Cuba lost its annual four-billion-dollar subsidies. This resulted in a profound economic crisis that pushed its citizens into an ongoing battle for survival. This dire situation gave rise to an atmosphere of turmoil and despair.

Out of desperation, individuals embarked on perilous sea voyages, attempting to reach the shores of the United States. Tragically, the odds were grim, with only one out of every four who attempted this treacherous journey reaching their destination alive.

On June 24th, Carlos found himself at a significant crossroads in his life. He was seated in a rigid and unwelcoming metal chair within the bustling Sagrado Corazon maternity hospital. The waiting room, a lively mosaic of sounds and people, held him captive. Leaning forward, he exuded a blend of restlessness and excitement, his right leg bouncing incessantly against the floor.

The door swung open, and a nurse came out. All eyes in the room turned on her, and the symphony of chatter yielded to her arrival.

A voice, clear and purposeful, pierced the silence. "Carlos…? Carlos Morales?"

The resonance of his name snapped Carlos from his seat, a reflexive response to its call.

"Right here!"

"Congratulations. It's a boy. Both mom and baby are doing great," the nurse said as Carlos approached, her tone warm and calming.

At that moment, relief cascaded through Carlos like a gentle tide, his body relaxing as a tender smile curved his lips. His gaze wandered with expectation. Tamara, Carlos's wife, had given birth to their firstborn.

"Thank you," he said.

"Follow me," the nurse instructed, setting things in motion. With a graceful pivot, she led the way through the hospital's interior. Carlos followed closely, keeping up with her brisk pace. An unspoken anticipation filled his actions as he moved through the corridors.

She stopped at a room's door, and with a gentle slowness, she swung it open. "Meet your son."

Carlos peeked inside, and a scene of profound tenderness captured his gaze — the baby cradled within the sanctuary of his mother's arms. Tamara was in her early twenties, petite, with short, highlight-dyed hair. Carlos entered the room tiptoeing, his footsteps careful as he approached her bed so as not to disturb the baby's precious sleep.

"Hey," he murmured, his voice a soft caress fading in the room.

Tamara met Carlos's gaze. Her lips curved into a gentle smile, an unspoken exchange of recognition passing between them. Her face radiated both fatigue and elation, embodying the trials and triumphs of childbirth.

"Hi."

Carlos leaned in, his lips pressed against her forehead in a chaste kiss. Then, his focus shifted to the heart of the room, the tiny being cocooned within his mother's embrace.

"Hey, little Johnny. It's me, daddy." The words whispered with such tenderness echoed through the room, marking the dawn of a new chapter.

Consumed by an overwhelming wave of joy, Carlos remained oblivious to the room's dilapidated state. Paint peeled away from the walls like fading memories, and the windows stood as mere frames, their glass missing or shattered. Amid this tableau of neglect, one artifact stood out — a rustic metal chair. Its form mirrored the uncomfortable one he had occupied in the waiting room.

A knowing smile curled his lips as he surveyed the scene. "Wow," he mused, a contemplative thought holding a hint of wry humor, "this is gonna be a long night."

The following day dawned, and the doctor granted the mother and baby their passage out of the hospital. They hailed a taxi, journeying to Tamara's dwelling nestled within the El Cerro neighborhood. Upon their arrival, sunlight wrapped around the house, casting gentle rays through the windows. As the front door squeaked open, a sense of homecoming filled the air. The mother stepped inside, her arms cradling the precious bundle of life, the baby whose arrival had transformed their world. Carlos followed closely, a bag in his grasp, his strides a blend of contented weariness. With a gentle click, he closed the door, shutting out the world beyond.

"We're home," she whispered.

Inside the bedroom, a haven of shared dreams and whispered promises, the mother found solace in a chair. Her countenance painted a portrait of gentleness as she cradled the baby to her breast. A maternal glow graced her visage, her eyes reflecting a mixture of awe and devotion. Within the room's embrace, the gentle rhythm of life resonated.

Yet, even amid this serene scene, the symphony of motherhood was punctuated by the wails of discontent. The baby's cries filled the room, a plaintive tune tugging at the mother's heartstrings. With a soothing touch, she shifted the baby to her other breast, an unspoken lullaby of comfort and reassurance.

Carlos entered the room, his presence a testament to his commitment as a partner and a father.

"How's it going?" he asked, his voice a blend of genuine concern and affection as his eyes traced the delicate dance of mother and child.

A momentary pause, a glance exchanged between two people bound by love and the shared journey of parenthood.

"Not too well," she said, her voice a whispered confession, conveying the unspoken challenges of the moment.

The baby's cries persisted, an insistent plea resonating with their frustration and helplessness.

"I know, I know," the mother cooed gently, her tone a soothing balm as she sought to quell the storm of tears. "Mommy doesn't have enough milk."

She gently adjusted the baby's position, a graceful movement of maternal instinct, ensuring comfort and nourishment. In response, the baby's cries faded, replaced by a peaceful calm.

"We need baby milk," the mother said, her voice tinged with a mixture of vulnerability and determination. "I'm not making enough."

In that moment, the room held within its walls not only the struggle of the present but also the promise of a challenging future. Carlos shed the residue of a restless night spent on the unyielding hospital chair, determination guiding his actions as he snatched up his wallet and keys.

"I'm going to the kitchen for the rationing book and to make a quick trip for food."

The rationing book was a government-issued document. The regime used this book to control the distribution of food and other limited resources. Each person was assigned a specific quota of items they could buy at a subsidized price, as outlined in the book's pages. While this system aimed to guarantee access to necessities, it also granted the government substantial authority over people's purchasing decisions and quantities. It provided a framework to manage shortages and maintain order, but it also restricted individual choice and fostered dependency on the government for basic needs.

Carlos pedaled his bike to the nearby food store just a few blocks away. The store's interior was dimly lit, with dust hanging in the air and the walls displaying the wear of time. Behind the counter, an aged and indifferent store attendant leaned with an air of detachment as if unaware of Carlos's arrival. Neglect seemed to permeate the atmosphere. Undeterred, Carlos approached the attendant.

"Got any baby milk?" Carlos asked.

The attendant's response was a somber shake of the head, a silent admission of scarcity.

Carlos moved on to another store, but again, his efforts yielded no results. He left the place empty-handed, his initial optimism dimming with each failed attempt. As he entered the third store, the familiar sight of dust-ridden shelves and empty spaces greeted him, the scene reminiscent of the previous establishments. However, a notable difference was exhibited in the attendant's demeanor. This one, a man in his early thirties, defied the Cuban norm of modest attire. Dressed in jeans and a t-shirt and sporting a Casio wristwatch, he exuded an air of contrast against the backdrop of scarcity. Behind the counter, he offered Carlos a warm smile, an unexpected kindness.

"Hi there!"

"Hey! Got baby milk?" Carlos asked.

"Are you drunk?"

"What?" Carlos frowned, puzzled.

"You have any idea what you're asking for?" The

attendant's tone carried an air of seasoned cynicism.

"Just baby milk. It's not like I'm asking for a steak, is it?"

The attendant's retort was laden with mockery. "Oh, boy. Someone's just landed on earth. Your first child, right?"

"Why?" Carlos asked, his voice filled with curiosity.

A wry smile touched the attendant's lips. "Cause you'd know that baby milk is kind of... a luxury item."

"Isn't it rationed by the government?"

"You just said it, rationed," the attendant said, gesturing quotation marks in the air. "It's one of those items we get through international donations... and all these donations go straight to the government."

The weight of reality settled on Carlos. "Shit! I really need baby milk... you're the third store I've been to. I don't know where else to go."

The attendant's eyes met Carlos's gaze, a flashing reflection of shared sorrow.

"Listen," the attendant's voice lowered conspiratorially, "there's a friend of a friend. He might be able to help you. A couple of blocks down, on Palatino Street, behind the Water Management building, ask for Luis 'the Tourist.' I don't have an address, but you'll find him."

"Thank you, man. I really appreciate it," Carlos said, heading for the store's door.

"Don't tell him I sent you."

"Got it," Carlos shouted as he exited the store.

Following the attendant's advice, Carlos embarked on a quest to find Luis, the enigmatic 'Tourist.' He walked down Palatino Street until he arrived at the Water Management building, where he encountered an aged figure resting on a worn chair by the sidewalk. Engaging in conversation with the old man, Carlos sought direction. A quick interaction ensued, and the old man signaled a nearby teenager. When the boy arrived, the old man whispered instructions into the boy's ear. The boy, summoned into action, headed off, and Carlos, in pursuit, followed the youthful guide into the narrow confines of a neighboring alley.

"Wait here," the boy said as he ventured further into the alley's depths.

After a brief wait, the teenager returned, accompanied by another man in his mid-thirties, dressed in blue jeans, a t-shirt, cap, and sunglasses. A thick golden chain hung from his neck. Whispering, the teenager says something to the man, and they both glanced at Carlos. A comforting pat from the man to the youth marked their parting.

"Luis?" Carlos asked as the man approached, his voice a mixture of hope and uncertainty.

The man scrutinized Carlos, his reply calculated with a purposeful delay. His dark sunglasses added an aura of mystery and intimidation to his figure, and his stern expression portrayed a serious business demeanor.

"You're not from around here, are you?" His voice was cold and inquisitive.

"Actually, yes... by the sports center," Carlos said.

His query hung in the air, charged with intrigue. "What is it you seek?"

"Baby milk."

Luis, his gaze vigilant, surveyed their surroundings before jerking a nod of agreement.

"That'll be ten."

"Okay," Carlos said, his hand delving into his pocket to retrieve his wallet. He got a 10-Cuban-Pesos note and handed it over to Luis.

Luis glanced at the bill and back to Carlos. "I meant ten dollars," Luis said, rejecting the money.

"You're kidding me, right? US dollars? That's illegal."

A surge of agitation laced Luis's voice as he countered, "And what exactly do you think you're doing now? You think this is legal?"

Caught in a tense moment, Carlos attempted to meet Luis's eyes, only to confront his reflection mirrored in Luis's sunglasses. A transient paralysis enveloped him as the weight of his situation bore down. The prospect of prison time loomed ominously, yet the urgency of nourishing his newborn overshadowed his fear. Carlos's gaze faltered, shifting to the ground. "You're right," he admitted, his voice tinged with embarrassment.

"Look, if you want baby milk, rice, beans, meat, clothes… anything, you need US dollars."

"How?" Carlos asked.

"You buy them."

"Where?"

"I can't help you with that. I just know they're trading 36 to 1," Luis said, a touch of warmth melting into his voice, a departure from his earlier frostiness.

"Are you serious? Thirty-six pesos for one measly dollar? That's almost what I make in a week as a crane operator."

"I know. You'll have to figure it out," Luis said before turning away, his footsteps fading.

As the man left, Carlos remained there in awe, letting his new reality sink in.

Carlos embarked on a journey as the sun kissed the horizon with the promise of a new day. He rode his bike along the highway known as 'Las Ocho Vias,' meaning the eight lines. His destination lay ahead, marked by the remnants of a broken road sign, discarded and forgotten. It had been down for months since an out-of-control vehicle crashed into it.

Carlos arrived at the broken sign and got off his bike. "I have better plans for you," he thought, taking deliberate steps to remove the aluminum plate from the steel bars.

After several hours, Carlos returned home with the sheet of metal. With meticulous resolve, he embarked on a creative endeavor. His skilled hands shaped the aluminum plate, guiding its transformation from a discarded road sign into an improvised oven. The result was a rectangular box with one side functioning as a door, its exterior adorned with the colors and letters of the road sign. This box stood as a testament to his resourcefulness, symbolizing his ability to turn challenges into opportunities.

Carlos positioned the box atop the stove and tested the fluidity of the door's movement. "This will work," he said, a proclamation directed at his craftsmanship and resilience.

Carlos returned to the last food store he visited. Standing next to the counter was the attendant who tipped him on finding Luis, 'the Tourist.'

"Hi, there," Carlos said.

A spark of recognition illuminated the attendant's eyes. "You're back!"

"Yeah, and thanks for your advice the other day," Carlos said in a tone of gratitude.

"I'm glad to help." A sincere smile appeared on the attendant's face.

Carlos leaned in, his voice shrouded in confidentiality, "Hey, I need some baking flour... off the books."

The attendant's gaze swiveled around, a cautious instinct guiding his actions. "It's 30 a pound."

"Cubans?"

"Mm-hmm!"

The attendant asked for a price ten times higher than the government's set rate. Ironically, government supplies either fell short or proved insufficient to meet the people's needs. Consequently, an underground market emerged, running alongside the official distribution channels and spreading across the entire island.

Carlos retrieved his rationing book, its pages offering a cover for the transaction about to unfold. With practiced subtlety, he tucked 30 Cuban pesos between its pages and placed the book on the counter. His voice, a mere whisper, formed the request, "Just one pound."

The attendant took the book and its concealed offering and, with a magician's ability, made the money disappear in his hand. He feigned annotating the transaction in the book before returning it to Carlos. Then, the man went to the back of the store and returned with a small paper bag.

"Anything else?" he asked as he placed the paper bag over the counter.

"That'll be all. Thank you," Carlos said, his words imbued with a blend of gratitude and discreet accomplishment.

Back in his kitchen, Carlos ventured on a culinary endeavor born of both necessity and ingenuity. With a measure of baking flour, he managed the formation of a dough, guided by a handwritten recipe on a scrap of paper.

He used an empty bottle to flatten the dough and a medium-size void of an emptied can to carve out circular portions destined for transformation. Then, he added some guava jelly to the center of each dough disc and folded the halves in harmonious unison, pressed together by the careful guidance of a fork's prongs. With two dozen pastries prepared, he placed them inside the aluminum box above the stove and turned the flame on.

Carlos gazed at the clock and back at the aluminum box. "You guys, hang in there. I'll be back soon."

Carlos returned to the kitchen twenty minutes later and opened the aluminum box.

"Yeah! You're ready," he said as he inspected the pastries and turned off the stove.

Carlos took the pastries out of the improvised oven and placed them on the table, letting them sit for a couple of minutes. He tossed one pastry onto a plate. "Shit," Carlos muttered, his burned thumb meeting his lips in a reflexive act of cooling relief.

Undeterred, he dissected the chosen treat and held it with a fork as a cautious puff of air dissipated the heat. The rookie baker took a small bite, a baptism of flavors to the waiting palate. "Hmmm! This is good."

Carlos placed the rest of the pastries on a plate and covered them with a clean kitchen towel. He secured the plate inside a wooden box hitched to his bike's rear and took off.

Carlos arrived at a crowded bus stop, got off the bike, and set up the bike stand. Amid the bustling congregation of hopeful travelers, Carlos found his haven.

"Pastries... guava pastries," he shouted to the crowd.

The first inquiry landed like a pebble in a pond, rippling through the crowd. "How much?"

"Three pesos," he replied, his fingers unfurling to reveal the numerical chorus.

"Give me two," a man said, sticking his hand into his pocket.

"Same for me," echoed another.

"I want one," a woman shouted from behind.

In the blink of an eye, Carlos found himself encircled by eager patrons, their appetites as voracious as their curiosity. Like leaves carried by the wind, the pastries vanished into the hands of those who sought their taste.

Back home, Carlos entered the bedroom, where his wife rocked the baby. He pulled a pack of bills and counted the money.

"Sixty-nine pesos," he announced, the notes crinkling like a chorus of congratulations in his hands. "In less than two hours. Can you believe it?" His voice brimmed with a kind of excitement only genuine accomplishment could evoke.

It was an achievement worth celebrating. In an era when a doctor earned a mere salary of 300 pesos per month, about ten pesos a day, Carlos had surpassed that in a fraction of the time. This experience unveiled his latent entrepreneurial spirit. Choosing this path could bring substantial rewards, but it also carried significant risks, especially in a society often punishing entrepreneurship with imprisonment.

Carlos's bakery venture soared like a rocket. The food store became his frequent stop, its attendant an unofficial partner in his mission. In hushed conversations, the attendant became his mentor, shedding light on the obscure route to getting the elusive US dollars.

With US dollars in his pocket, Carlos rode his bike to Luis' neighborhood. A few blocks' ride turned into a long maze as Carlos altered his course for alternative routes every time he saw cops ahead, a dance of evasion as intricate as any choreography. He knew carrying US dollars was a perilous endeavor, a venture more treacherous than trafficking cocaine. After arriving at the alley, he got to see Luis.

Carlos returned home. He entered, pulling his bike as he sang a song.

"Hm, what're you up to?" Tamara asked, her voice carried a curious note.

Carlos rested his bike against the wall and walked toward his wife. He kissed her and took off his backpack. With a triumphal expression, he opened his backpack and pulled out a can of baby formula.

Her embrace enveloped him, a gesture of both gratitude and awe. "Where did you find this?" she whispered, her eyes gleaming with wonder.

For weeks, Carlos's enterprise unfolded beneath the surface of everyday life. Amid it all, a father's devotion endured as an unspoken pledge to provide for his child's sustenance, overcoming hurdles to ensure it.

One afternoon, Carlos went to the store for more flour. Another attendant presided behind the counter, his look familiar. The untucked shirt and wearied countenance marked him as the former attendant from the first food store.

"Hello," Carlos greeted, his voice a mask of casual curiosity.

The man's response, devoid of enthusiasm, echoed the lethargy of their surroundings. "How can I help you?" he inquired, perching like a spectator of his own disinterest.

"The usual attendant... is he off today?" Carlos inquired, his words infused with an air of feigned innocence.

"He is no longer working here."

Carlos maintained a veneer of curiosity. "Transferred to another store?"

A moment's pause, pregnant with tension. The man gave Carlos an unpleasant look. "He was arrested."

A shock of realization surged through Carlos, though he concealed it with the mastery of a seasoned performer. Then he reacted, acting surprised. "Really? He seemed like a nice guy." And with these parting words, Carlos retreated, leaving the store.

As he returned home, Carlos's head was a thunderstorm of reflection and caution. He set out on another baking endeavor with the remaining flour, finding refuge from his inner turmoil in the rhythmic motions of his hands and the familiar fragrance of dough.

Aware of the watchful eyes of the authorities, Carlos comprehended that the risks had escalated significantly. The police, meticulous in their scrutiny, might be amassing evidence, tracking patterns, and forging connections. "They're biding their time for the right moment to dismantle the entire network," he pondered, his thoughts a strategic chessboard. His movements had to be cautious, his actions scrupulous.

His persistent determination materialized into a structured plan. Every gram of flour would be transformed into pastries to get rid of any evidence at home. "Finish this flour; keep a low profile for now," he resolved, the pathway ahead clear in his mind. "Then, a new supplier, a new link in the chain."

Bringing along the last batch of pastries, Carlos reached another crowded bus stop, resolute in selling his stock. With honed intuition, he scanned his surroundings attentively, analyzing every movement and glance for potential threats.

The inventory dwindled rapidly, like sand slipping through the hourglass. Half of his wares found new homes in a matter of moments, his makeshift bakery drawing hungry patrons like moths to a flame. Yet, amid the transient joy of his brisk sales, an imminent threat materialized at the corner of his vision: two figures in uniform, a harbinger of potential trouble.

One cop saw the commotion and alerted his partner. The two men started walking fast toward Carlos. Time distorted, the seconds elongating as Carlos's heart raced. The law's emissaries drew closer, their purpose unspoken but palpable. As a customer extended his payment, Carlos had to decide in a heartbeat between profit and freedom. Ignoring a customer, Carlos pushed his bike and ran through the crowd.

"Wait! Your money," the customer shouted.

The cops chased Carlos. As soon as he cleared the crowd, Carlos jumped on the bike and took off. The pursuit unfolded with relentless intensity. A glance over his shoulder revealed the persistent advance of one determined cop, an embodiment of the law's pursuit. Carlos's grip on the handlebars tightened as he pressed forward, pedaling faster.

And then, a cruel twist of fate. A pothole materialized like a phantom right in front of him, too close for an evasive maneuver. In a desperate move, he tried to jump the hole with the bike. Victory was partial; the bike's front wheel cleared the chasm, but the rear wheel collided, throwing the precious cargo out of the box.

As the pastries scattered on the cracked pavement, Carlos scanned the road ahead, his mind anticipating the next move in a fraction of a second. The next intersection on the left was a downhill street. Carlos pivoted left into the oncoming flow of traffic, a calculated gamble as the world around him erupted in disarray. In an instinctive reaction, the driver stepped hard on the brake and pulled the steering wheel to the left. His panicked eyes widened.

The tires squealed, and Carlos barely avoided a collision. With the driver's swerve, the car jolted toward a halt, a ballet of fear on the asphalt stage. It finally stopped, blocking the cop who landed both hands on the vehicle's hood. He looked at the driver, rage pouring from his eyes.

Downhill, Carlos gained speed and left the cops behind. Consumed by frustration, the cop kicked the side of the vehicle as he watched Carlos get away. Carlos turned at the next corner and disappeared.

Breathless but alive, Carlos arrived home and pulled his bike inside. The crescendo of his heartbeats gradually subsided, the rhythm of his pulse echoing the lingering thrill of his escape. A quick shower rinsed off the remnants of his flight, and a fresh set of clothes provided a shield against the turmoil he had left in his wake. He grabbed a set of clean clothes and threw them inside his backpack.

The comforting embrace of home provided a fleeting moment of solace prior to departure. On his way out, he kissed Tamara and the baby's forehead. "I'm going to Mom's house for a couple of days," he said.

"Is everything alright?" Her voice held a note of concern, her intuition finely attuned to the shifts in his demeanor.

"Hope so," he said, his words laden with a mix of reassurance and unease. "But the guy at the food store got busted."

Carlos waited at the bus stop. He was heading to his family house in El Calvario, a town located ten kilometers south of Havana's iconic Capitol building.

Established during Spanish colonization, El Calvario was known for its tranquil and hospitable character. Its area covered just a square kilometer. At the center of this charming settlement stood Havana's oldest church. This unpretentious sanctuary had once been the focal point of grand Catholic processions. Devotees from various places converged here to partake in the splendid celebrations.

However, in the present day, the small chapel stands shuttered, its doors sealed with nails, and a portion of its roof missing. These decaying remnants bear witness to the stories shared by the town's elderly residents. Today, El Calvario has assumed a distinct role, one far removed from peace and festivity. A few blocks away from the church, the headquarters of the Western army casts a shadow. Its military personnel have taken control of the colonial edifice, which was formerly used to house a Catholic seminary.

"Damn it! Two hours waiting and no sign of the bus," Carlos muttered, his frustration growing.

Across the street, two police officers halted a pedestrian carrying a bag. They coerced him into revealing the contents of his pack, emptying his pockets, and removing his shoes on the sidewalk. Oblivious to the scene, other passersby continued on their paths. They had gotten used to these regular searches. After a while, the officers set the man free and took another hapless individual into custody to repeat the intimidating ritual. Above them, towering several meters high, the government had erected an immense billboard adorned with a portrait of Fidel Castro, the Comandante, with the phrase, "In my house, I rule." It stood out as the sole painted facade on the entire avenue.

Carlos looked at the policemen, his gaze intense and piercing. From there, he shifted his attention to the billboard. A surge of anger coursed through him, contorting his lips and furrowing his brow. In an act of defiance, he leaned forward, spat on the ground, and turned his focus to the bustling street.

A bus appeared on the horizon. It moved at high speed, zigzagging through potholes and cyclists on the road. Carlos saw the vehicle and retreated several paces, creating a safe distance from the sidewalk.

Almost instantly, a multitude of people swarmed the bus stop. They were waiting, too, scattered under the surrounding trees to escape the relentless heat. The crowd was a turbulent sea of people, with each individual vying for a prime position in the upcoming boarding frenzy. The desire to be first on board was clear, transcending age, gender, and physical limitations. Pregnant and disabled people, and even small children, held no sway. It was the urban jungle, the survival of the fittest.

The oncoming vehicle displayed no intention of slowing down. The bus resembled a can of sardines crammed with passengers. Bodies spilled out from its doors and windows, a clear sign of the excessive crowding. Within this mix were youthful faces seeking excitement alongside regular commuters compelled by lack of choice.

Black smoke billowed from the exhaust as the driver pressed the pedal. The vehicle passed without making the slightest attempt to stop, and many people chased after it at full speed; perhaps the red light at the intersection would make it halt.

Carlos watched the unfolding spectacle before him. He would have sprinted after the metallic beast, but not this time. These were special days, for his firstborn, Juan Carlos, had entered the world. And this baby's arrival had captured his father's undivided attention.

Carlos stared at the bus as it ignored the red light to escape the pursuing crowd. It narrowly avoided hitting unsuspecting pedestrians crossing the intersection. In that instant, a profound realization swept over Carlos. His eyes widened, his bewildered stare became fixed, and he couldn't breathe for a second. The episode left him stunned.

In the blink of an eye, a montage of vivid images raced through his mind, unfolding like a memory-crafted film. Each frame unveiled a chapter of his life, each more steeped in misery than the last. Indeed, any recollection of the past brought a burden of longing and sadness for what had been lost. The lack of essentials like food, clothing, and footwear wasn't the only issue; respect, freedom, and dreams were also deteriorating. The oppressive fear of police harassment has made a simple walk through the streets a harrowing ordeal. Knowing that the future would be worse than the past heralded a gloomy tomorrow.

"Is this what my son's future holds? I can't live in this shitty country anymore," Carlos weighed in his thoughts as he walked away.

Hours later, Carlos arrived at his house in El Calvario. The weight of his frustration surpassed the weariness of his seven-kilometer march. Seeking solace, he made his way to the kitchen. He mixed two tablespoons of sugar into a glass of cold water and quenched his parched throat with the sweet mixture. He wanted to clear his head, so he went for a walk around the neighborhood. An hour later, he returned carrying discarded pieces of lumber salvaged from a nearby construction site. Carlos embarked on a task with a well-defined goal in mind—cleaning, measuring, and sawing the wood he had collected.

In the following days, Carlos remained consumed by his solitary endeavor. Enveloped in a veil of silence, he delved deep into his thoughts, oblivious to the outside world. Only two subjects occupied his mind: his cherished son and the project taking shape before him. Carlos's focused demeanor and the visible progress of his work aroused the curiosity of his relatives. They became intrigued and eager for insight into Carlos's work.

"Son, what're you up to?" Carmen asked.

"A raft to get out of here! What else is there to do?" His sarcastic tone infuriated his mother.

"Stop spouting nonsense, or I'll set that... that thing on fire!" The mother's startled reaction mirrored the near-inevitable response she had expected from her son.

Carmen's reaction was not unwarranted, as she knew about the clandestine departures. She had witnessed the political oppression suffered by those captured attempting to flee the island. Even worse, she was aware of the disappearances at sea. Carmen had a profound understanding of her two sons, Carlos and Roberto. Carlos possessed an impulsive nature, a blend of skill and stubbornness resembling a ticking time bomb almost impossible to defuse once activated. Conversely, Roberto exhibited a reserved and methodical manner, signified by reticence. He had the patience of a skilled hunter, holding out for the ideal moment to strike. Although Roberto remained distant from Carlos's project, Carmen sensed he wouldn't stay detached for much longer.

News of the incident soon reached Gerardo's ears, eliciting an enthusiastic response.

Gerardo has always maintained a close bond with the brothers' family. In his childhood, Gerardo endured the ruthless brutality inflicted by the police upon those who dared to oppose the regime.

On April 1st, 1980, a bold incident unfolded when a group of five individuals commandeered a stolen bus to break into the Peruvian embassy in Havana. The bus was rammed into the consulate's main entrance, allowing access to the premises. Amid the chaos, security guards positioned on either side of the gate fired a barrage of shots to halt the vehicle's progress. Despite their efforts, the bus breached the embassy grounds. Tragically, a guard accidentally shot and killed his colleague amid the crossfire.

In response, the Cuban government demanded the immediate surrender of the intruders, while those within the embassy sought political asylum. The Peruvian government granted asylum, defying the Cuban regime's requests. In a retaliatory move, the island's authorities withdrew police protection from the embassy.

The news spread like wildfire throughout the population, igniting an unstoppable fervor. Within a week, around 10,000 people invaded the embassy premises. They occupied the backyard, parking lots, roofs, trees, and even the fence protecting the property. It was impossible to contain this swelling crowd in such a small space. The Cuban government found itself grasping for a solution. Initially, the police blocked all access points to the embassy and its surrounding areas. Then, Castro announced anyone desiring to depart the country could do so. However, this was easier said than done since the path to freedom was fraught with obstacles.

Regular commercial flights between Cuba and the USA were nonexistent. In a joint effort, both governments struck an agreement permitting US residents to use their own vessels to pick up relatives from the island. Immediately, the Cuban exiles in Miami mobilized boat fleets, embarking on a monumental mission to retrieve their loved ones from the island. This historic endeavor came to be known as the Mariel boatlift, a maritime bridge spanning from Key West, Florida to the port of Mariel, in Cuba. From April 15th to October 31st, 1980, a staggering fleet of about 1,700 small and medium-sized boats took part in this exodus.

The global community viewed the Mariel exodus as a humanitarian endeavor to reunite Cubans with their overseas families. Yet, for the Cuban regime, this migration presented an opportune moment for a nationwide purge. Capitalizing on the situation, they orchestrated the expulsion of a diverse range of individuals. This included dangerous criminals, individuals with mental health conditions, and those with homosexual preferences, derogatorily labeled as "social scum" by the communist government.

This forced departure affected around 125,000 people who sought refuge in neighboring nations. The government also launched an extensive repressive campaign to stifle any form of dissent. Gerardo found himself ensnared in the middle of this crackdown, becoming an unfortunate victim of the regime's authoritarian rule.

Gerardo's dreams of becoming a doctor were shattered when his school denied him the opportunity to pursue higher education. He was only fourteen years old. Sadly, he wasn't alone in facing this predicament. Many students saw their educational journeys disrupted because of their parents' intention to emigrate. The repression extended beyond just denying Gerardo's educational path. Despite his youth, he endured psychological torment, compelled by authorities to endure grueling interrogations at a nearby police station alongside his father.

Despite years of government-imposed obstacles that kept Gerardo's family from leaving the country, he held onto his longing to escape the island. When Carlos started his daring plan, Gerardo saw a tangible path to realizing his dream.

Carlos's raft had been the major topic of conversation in Carmen's house for weeks. Carmen responded to her son's project with hostility, including her threat to set the raft on fire. The tension affected Carmen's health, leading to anxiety attacks, a rapid heart rate, and high blood pressure. As the situation escalated, Roberto stepped in to mediate and bring resolution.

"Look! Mom's health isn't the best. I think you should take a break and let the dust settle, and I'll help you plan the trip," he said.

Carlos remained silent, his gaze fixed upon the raft he had built before returning his attention to Roberto.

"Okay," he conceded, his voice laced with apprehension.

The brothers moved the raft to the storage room, hoping to put the matter to rest. However, Gerardo, with his relentless banter, kept raising the topic day after day, forcing Roberto to intervene.

"Gerardo, knock it off with my brother's crazy idea. It's not funny..."

"Bro, the raft is no laughing matter!" Gerardo interrupted his friend. "Things are going to get worse here. There is no food; we are starving. We have to rely on the black market just to eat. We are living with a foot in the jail's door. Soon, those who aren't sick or dead will be in prison."

Roberto fell silent, the weight of Gerardo's words sinking in. He understood all too well the painful truth embedded within them.

"This is serious," he thought, his mind consumed by his friend's depressing predictions and the unexpected direction the conversation had taken.

"Okay, Gerardo, let's assess the situation, but don't add fuel to the fire for now."

"You're right. He's made too much noise. Good thing no one takes him seriously, 'cause he's always messing around. If not, someone would've called the cops by now."

"I'll talk to him. We can't allow him to leave alone or with the first person he finds," Roberto said.

"I hadn't thought about that, but you're right. Your brother is impulsive, and this journey requires careful preparation."

"Very well. Let's research about the trip so we can make a plan," Roberto suggested. "But I want to make it clear now... I'm not leaving. I don't want to leave my mom and grandma. Besides, this is my country!"

"What country are you talking about?" Gerardo challenged in disagreement. "The government treats us like second-class citizens. You're not allowed to enter a fine restaurant or a nightclub or spend a night at a hotel unless you are a foreign tourist. We live in social segregation and have no rights just for being Cubans."

"That's true," Roberto admitted, his voice tinged with sadness, "but I want to be here when this shitty government falls."

From that moment on, they became avid listeners to the whispers and anecdotes surrounding the rafters. They sought friends and acquaintances, seeking any contacts with those who had attempted the perilous journey but had failed. It was a sensitive subject, and their inquiries had to be discreet, making their quest more difficult.

Both men immersed themselves in the narratives, absorbing the stories of those who had triumphed against the odds. They learned about the immense challenges and setbacks they had encountered along the way. Equally important were the tales of those who had faced unfortunate fates, shedding light on the mistakes that had cost them their lives. Gathering this knowledge became crucial to their mission as they strove to navigate the treacherous path ahead and evade the tragic pitfalls that had befallen so many others.

During those days, Raul, a new student transferred to Roberto and Gerardo's classroom, emerged as a fearless figure. Like many of his peers, the young man harbored an intense opposition to the government.

"I worked as a bartender at the Convention Palace," Raul told his new friends. "The sheer amount of food wasted there, while people are starving, is criminal. And they won't let you take any leftovers."

Raul's stories were not unfamiliar, but they acted as a catalyst, accelerating the bond forming between the future crew members. By sharing their outrage and experiences, they developed an unspoken understanding that strengthened their connection.

Days turned into weeks, and their friendship grew stronger. Together, they embarked on fishing trips, ventured out on exciting outings, and indulged in small gatherings accompanied by their girlfriends and wives, forging the foundation of a team built to withstand future challenges.

When their bond seemed unbreakable, they broached the delicate subject. They joked about the news on Radio Martí, the clandestine radio station broadcasting from the United States. It constituted their only connection to the outside world, providing updates on Cubans rescued at sea. Merely admitting to listening to Radio Martí could lead to arrests and fines. Later, as they grew more comfortable with one another, they wove snippets of this forbidden topic into their conversations, injecting a touch of humor.

"Did you hear? The US Coast Guard rescued another group yesterday... what are we waiting for?"

As time passed, these casual comments about escaping on a raft became more frequent, revealing the underlying seriousness of their intentions. One evening, during an impromptu gathering at Carlos's house, Gerardo turned to Raul with a sense of purpose.

"Dude... wanna join our team?" Gerardo asked, his voice carrying a mix of hope and determination.

"Sure! Just tell me when and where!" Raul's response came without hesitation, his conviction clear. It looked like he had been expecting the invitation.

Carlos, Roberto, and Gerardo exchanged glances, their smiles conveying their shared excitement. Gerardo stepped closer to Raul, placing his right hand on his shoulder.

"Welcome to the team," Gerardo said, his voice brimming with camaraderie.

At that moment, Raul became part of the close-knit research squad. Later that night, Gerardo beckoned Raul outside the house, away from other attendants, and explained their plans more seriously.

With the help of a friend at the sports institute's library, Gerardo got a list of textbooks related to nautical sports and sailing in particular. This permitted them to conduct an exhaustive theoretical investigation, as practical education was unattainable. In Cuba, boating was a privilege reserved for the government elite and foreign tourists. Therefore, their attention turned to thorough analytical groundwork, understanding it would guide them through the hazardous journey ahead.

One late afternoon, Carlos and Roberto stood in front of their house enjoying the cool breeze when Ivan, a family friend, approached.

"Yo, my man!" Ivan greeted Carlos, his tone overly affectionate. "Take me with you!"

Carlos raised an eyebrow, feigning confusion. "Where?"

"To the other side, ya know. I wanna get out of here."

"Everyone wants to leave," Carlos said, his voice tinged with resignation.

"True, but you're actually doing something about it."

"Huh?" Carlos put on a facade of incomprehension.

"C'mon, man..." Ivan rebutted, his tone mocking. "I've worked with your mother for years and know her very well. She's worried because of what you're doing. I'm not stupid."

Carlos attempted to deflect the seriousness of the conversation. "You know me, Ivan. I'm always bullshitting."

"Bullshitting or not, I just wanna say, if you ever need someone, count on me," Ivan said with a wry smile.

Carlos remained silent, his gaze shifting toward his brother who had been listening from the sidelines. Sure enough, the team needed another member but couldn't ignore their concerns. If Ivan had heard about their plans, others might have too. The sensitive nature of their endeavor urged them to exercise caution and discretion.

Ivan, in his early thirties, was short in stature with a robust build. His contagious sense of humor could easily crack even the sternest of individuals, leaving them with a smile. He relished moments spent sharing stories and drinks with his friends. Like Carlos, Ivan's major worry was providing food for his wife and his little daughter. To fulfill this responsibility, Ivan had made the tough choice of family separation, knowing it would come with significant sacrifices.

A few days later, Ivan once again approached the brothers with his characteristic friendly nature.

"Yo, don't forget our chat," he said.

"I won't, but remember, this isn't..." Carlos hesitated, unable to finish the sentence.

"I got two tractor tubes at home; the big ones used in the rear tires. One is damaged, but the other is in good shape, just missing the air valve. Also, I served in the Navy during my

Military Service, so I have experience at sea," Ivan said with enthusiasm.

Carlos paused, his eyes narrowing as he contemplated the offer. "Okay but listen. We'll talk to the others and see what they say. For now, keep those tubes safe."

The brothers knew Ivan very well and regarded him as a viable addition to the future crew. After all, the young men had determined that five members (four oarsmen and one helmsman) were the ideal number the crew needed to operate the boat. Soon after, the two brothers discussed the matter with Gerardo and Raul.

"Ivan wants to join the group," Carlos said, starting the impromptu meeting at Carmen's house in El Calvario. "He was in the Navy, so I think he's a good fit."

"I don't know." Raul leaned back in his chair as a deep breath filled his lungs. "You know him better than me, but remember, 'chivas' are everywhere."

Raul's response revealed the profound fear and mistrust deeply rooted in Cuban society, especially among younger people. Undercover informants, often referred to as 'chivas,' were present in the community, reporting any questionable action in the vicinity to the authorities. Like a symptomless plague, it was impossible to identify who carried the disease.

"Nah, this guy is cool," Carlos said, seeing his reflection in Ivan.

"I think you're right," Gerardo agreed. "Besides, the dude was a sailor. We've known him for years, and he's going through the same shit we are."

"Sure!" Roberto said. "We can trust him. Plus, we need five men on the team, so you guys can take breaks and switch off."

Roberto remained steadfast in his decision to stay on the island. His primary concern was supporting his brother and friends in achieving their goals.

The assembly was brief and to the point. They deliberated for some time before arriving at a conclusion.

"If you're good with him, then so am I," Raul said.

"Then... do we let him in?" Roberto asked.

They looked at each other, and a sense of understanding passed between them.

"Yes!" they concurred.

Later that day, Carlos visited Ivan, eager to deliver the group's long-awaited decision.

"Are you ready, partner?" Carlos extended his right hand for a shake. "Welcome aboard!"

As they shook hands, Ivan couldn't contain his enthusiasm, and he pulled Carlos into a tight embrace, looking up at the heavens with gratitude.

The next day, Ivan brought the airlock inner tubes to Carmen's house and gave them to Carlos. Carlos examined the tubes and stashed them in the attic, close to the unfinished vessel.

By now, the team had gathered ample knowledge about the forthcoming challenges. It was time to design a vessel to accommodate a crew of five comprising four rowers and one helmsman. And because of Roberto's determination to stay in the country, his cousin Didier would fill the fifth spot.

Although he was a mere eighteen years old, Didier, Ramon's son, emerged as the perfect candidate and displayed remarkable enthusiasm for the concept. Beyond his familial ties, he also functioned as Carlos's collaborator in his fishing endeavors and maintained exceptional physical fitness. The lone concern rested with Sonia, his mother, who exhibited a propensity for impulsive behavior and excessive protectiveness. The team members feared Sonia could disclose their plans to the authorities to safeguard her son from the perils of the expedition. Given Sonia's potential for hostility, Didier felt uneasy and maintained some distance from the group.

————————⟨⟨✢⟩⟩————————

Summer, 1992.

Starting with the rustic shell fashioned by Carlos, Roberto embarked on a journey of creativity. Possessing an ardent fondness for drawing, he drafted several raft prototypes, dedicating himself to their constant improvement. Through persistent endeavors and several days of unwavering labor, he finally envisioned the vessel required for their purpose. Each pencil stroke bore purpose, translating the precise dimensions of the forthcoming construction onto a 1:20 scale. An inch on paper symbolized twenty inches in the physical realm. Upon accomplishing his creation, Roberto beamed with pride as he presented it to his compatriots.

"You're kidding. Two sails?" Carlos asked, his eyes widening in disbelief.

"Yeah, we need two sails," Roberto said, his tone serene and confident.

"But why two? Isn't one enough?" Carlos persisted.

"If we're doing this, we'll do it right," Roberto said. "Columbus reached America using sails. The bigger sail will pull the raft, while the smaller one will help reduce the turbulence behind the mainsail."

"Hmm, I don't know. That seems like it's way too heavy," Raul said.

"That's true, but keep in mind, you guys only gotta carry her for a bit. Once at sea, she will carry all of you for several days." Roberto's explanation resonated with conviction. "Ah, one more thing! We gotta baptize her."

"Baptize her?" Raul asked.

"Yes, we need to name her and stop using the word 'raft.' You never know who might overhear us," Roberto said.

"Yes, yes, you're right. How about 'The Artifact'?" Gerardo asked.

"Hmm!" Roberto's brow furrowed, expressing his dissatisfaction. "Sounds fishy."

Carlos, rising from his seat, shouted, "Esperanza! We'll call her Esperanza."

"That's right! I like it," they agreed.

"From now on, we'll talk about Esperanza as a friend," Roberto concluded, sealing their decision.

Beyond its frequent usage as a female name, Esperanza meant 'hope' in their native language, encapsulating the very core of their endeavor. This intangible power forged a deep connection among these youthful companions, driving them forward toward a united goal.

As discussions unfolded, technical queries emerged as they sought to understand the attributes of the novel raft: "What's this?" "How will it work?" etc. Each query found its fitting response, appeasing all engaged parties. The design laid the groundwork for a structured workflow, and the prospective crew members were armed with the requisite understanding to fulfill their roles. A comprehensive blueprint for crafting the vessel was in their possession, accompanied by a clear comprehension of the essential materials required.

However, another challenge soon presented itself. A secure, private place was essential for crafting the boat in secret.

Carmen's house in El Calvario appeared to be the ideal location because of its spaciousness. Yet, a significant drawback was the lack of privacy. The house held the sole telephone in town, attracting constant visits from neighbors who needed to make phone calls. This was a massive inconvenience that could not be ignored.

"An attic would be a solution," Roberto proposed.

"Let's build one," Carlos said enthusiastically.

It proved to be the most suitable remedy to maintain their activities in secrecy. Given the housing shortage, many Cubans built habitable attics, making it common to find three-generation families living under a single roof.

Amid the challenges of acquiring construction materials, the brothers gathered discarded wood from a nearby construction site. With Raul and Gerardo's help, they built a spacious and sturdy attic, allowing them to proceed with their work unhindered.

Four future members of the crew gathered at Raul's house. From left to right: Gerardo, Raul, Roberto, and Carlos

ESPERANZA
(HOPE)

Escale 1:20

Leyend
1. Farm tractor neumatic (1 x 6' diameter)
2. Autobus neumatics (4 x 4' diameter)
3. Wooden Estructure
4. Keels or Cetreboards (2)
5. Rudder
6. Oars (4)
7. Mast
8. Mainsail
9. Small Sail / Jib
10. Tensors (3): Forestay (1), Backstay (2)

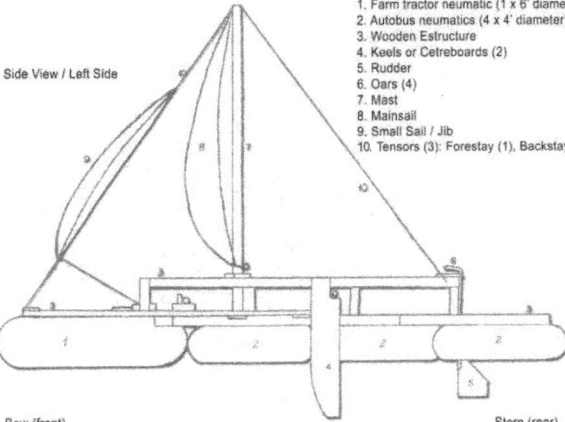

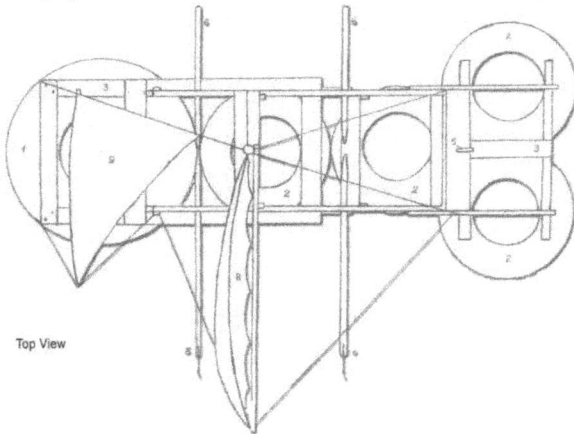

Side View / Left Side

Bow (front)

Stern (rear)

Top View

Esperanza (Hope). Side view (top) and top view (bottom). Designed by Roberto. Note: 1:20 represents the scale of the original drawing. This graphic has been reduced for editing purposes.

3

THE POINT OF NO RETURN

Time continued its endless march, running deeper into August.

One night, Roberto was returning home as the clock drew near midnight. He was tired after spending the entire day at the sports institute, but he still made the time to visit his girlfriend. It had been a long day, and exhaustion weighed heavily upon him. He arrived at a bus stop near the intersection of Vía Blanca and Palatino avenues and settled onto a bench, placing his school backpack between his feet. There, he patiently waited, his eyes scanning the area for any sign of movement. The streets were deserted; there were no signs of life.

As the moments passed, the minutes stretched out, seemingly prolonging their duration. The landscape appeared like a three-dimensional photograph with scarce lighting, casting an eerie ambiance over the night.

Over an hour crawled by, and finally, a glimmer of light emerged in the distance. The approaching vehicle's sluggish pace captured Roberto's attention. Along the Vía Blanca Avenue, known for reckless driving, this unusual moderation stood out. Roberto's eyes shifted toward the car, and as it drew nearer, he recognized it—it was a gray Mercedes-Benz van, none other than the dreaded Special Brigade.

The Special Brigade, a formidable military detachment assigned for civil affairs, operated under the umbrella of the national police. Its primary mission was to quell popular demonstrations and maintain control. Meticulously selected for their stature and muscular frames, these soldiers undergo arduous training in martial arts. Each patrol comprised seven well-armed soldiers and they used modern police minivans to enhance their mobility. They also employed military trucks and buses for mass transportation in situations demanding greater numbers. Cunningly, to deceive the foreign press and international opinion, members of these special forces often disguised themselves in civilian attire.

Roberto's heart raced as he secretly watched the patrol vehicle crawling past him. Uncertain of whether to flee or sit still, his breath hitched with anxiety as he saw the car executing a sudden U-turn and speeding up straight toward him.

"Shit! They're onto me."

The van's sliding side door was already wide open, and, with a screech, it came to a stop just a few steps from Roberto.

In a swift assault maneuver, several agents emerged, surrounding the young man.

"What's in the bag?" The captain asked, his tone demanding, while another agent seized Roberto's bag and checked its contents.

"School stuff."

The officer persisted in his scrutiny, resolute in his quest for incriminating evidence against Roberto.

"Books, notebooks, pencils..." the agent listed while dropping items on the sidewalk. "Eh... what's this?" he asked, his tone shifted to an accusatory one as he held up a small glass container.

"Perfume," the young man said. His relaxed demeanor belied the anxiety bubbling up within him.

"How'd you get it?"

"From a street vendor."

Roberto's response was an evasion commonly used to protect black market vendors. This underground economy, sprawling across the island, was a lifeline sustaining Cubans' survival.

"Come with us!" the captain said, his irritation palpable. He knew the words "from a street vendor" usually marked the end of an investigation for lack of leads.

The agents escorted Roberto to the van.

"Hands against the vehicle," one guard said.

Roberto pressed his palms against the car while another officer kicked his legs apart. The detainee submitted as the agent conducted a thorough pat-down search.

"Get in the car!"

As Roberto got into the vehicle, he saw two other detainees sitting on the floor, realizing he was not the only one under arrest. The van drove off the wide avenue and navigated through the narrow streets of the city. Roberto fought to suppress the mounting fear within him. His heart leaped into his throat and his hands turned cold and clammy as a thought of imprisonment came to him. It would not be his first time behind bars since he had been there twice for insubordination while in the Army, but that was just for a few days. However, on this occasion, the stakes were higher. If the police opted to search his house and found the raft, his family could be implicated. Besides, it was not uncommon for those caught purchasing goods through the black market to face a two-year prison sentence.

The van made its way to a police station in a neighborhood called El Canal within the Cerro municipality. Once inside the station, the agents led Roberto into a room and left him there. Minutes later, the captain entered and began his interrogation.

"You know the one who sold you the perfume, right?" the officer asked with an inquisitive tone.

With feigned calm, Roberto maintained a relaxed demeanor, his testimony unchanged. "No, I bumped into him on the street."

"So, why'd you buy it?"

"Because it was cheap," Roberto said, his tone taking on an unexpected touch of jest, infuriating the captain.

"Even if it was a gift, you shouldn't have bought it," the officer shouted in Roberto's face. Roberto's eyes flicked to the agent's left wrist and noticed the Casio watch.

Casio watches were off-limits to Cubans. They were only available in foreign tourist shops or through clandestine vendors. The officer embodied the hypocrisy of all Communist leaders, epitomizing the proverb, "do as I say, not as I do." The urge to inquire about the watch's origin tempted Roberto, but prudence prevailed.

He stood there, silent, using the lack of words as his protest against the humiliation he felt.

Roberto recognized the malicious intent behind this provocation. The officer intended to elicit a complaint, a pretext to throw him into a cell and subject him to a beating. After the battering, they would confine him and patiently wait for the bruises and swelling to subside, avoiding any potential allegation of abuse due to lack of evidence.

Endless hours ensued, laden with a pervasive gloomy atmosphere. The interrogation had concluded, and the clacking of a typewriter filled the air, the sound bouncing off the precinct's walls. But Roberto remained oblivious, his mind consumed by a more pressing worry.

"Are they gonna search the house? They will stumble upon the raft."

The officer on duty interrupted Roberto's thoughts, extending a form to him. "Sign here! You're free to go, but you'll have to pay a forty-pesos fine, and the perfume will be confiscated."

It was around three in the morning. The streets lay dark and deserted as Roberto made his way home. Gerardo's words, spoken over a year ago, echoed in Roberto's mind, "We are living with a foot in the jail's door."

His slow walk, downcast gaze, and hands deep in his pockets conveyed not just concern but also a profound sadness. He understood that living under such harassment and repression had become unbearable. He then accepted, with a heavy heart, that he must do what he had never wanted to do: leave his country.

Following the incident, the group's efforts gained momentum. With Roberto's commitment, he transitioned from being solely the team's organizer to becoming another member of the expedition. Carlos, who always stood out for his ingenuity, built the four oars using slender tree branches. Days later, the siblings cut two bigger branches. They crafted the mast and the boom out of these two larger pieces.

They also repurposed their trusty camping tent, a faithful companion on many fishing excursions, to create the sails and came up with a clever method using rings, ropes, and a pulley to enhance the sails' maneuverability.

The mainsail was triangular. Its canvas spread almost eight feet wide and ten feet tall. The vertical side of the sail was fitted with a carefully crafted seam, forming a cylindrical pocket, which effortlessly slid onto the mast to fasten the sail. The boom, a horizontal rod positioned at the mast's base, allowed the crew to control the sail. The sail's foot featured cleverly affixed rings linking the canvas to the boom, enabling the crew to deploy or stow the mainsail with ease. At the boom's far end, a pulley would allow the crew to deploy the mainsail by pulling a rope. With the mainsail retracted, the crew could raise and secure the boom to the mast. This would facilitate the mast and sails transfer. Finally, the mast's lower end would rest on a ball bearing fixed to the raft structure. This would allow the mast to rotate for better sail functionality.

To enhance the mast's sturdiness, three ropes (two backstays and one forestay) would anchor the mast to the boat. The two backstays would run from the mast's top to the raft's stern, while the forestay would tie the mast to the raft's bow. This last rope would also serve as a secondary mast, holding the smaller sail.

The smaller sail, called the jib, mirrored the mainsail's design, though it was simpler in construction. Unlike the mainsail, it was not attached to a wooden mast. Instead, the forestay line would keep this sail upright. The brothers use a 1.5-meter bamboo stick as a boom, fastened to the sail's lower edge to keep it unfurled. It did not have a system of rings and a pulley like the mainsail. The jib could be retracted by rolling the canvas around the boom and fastening it to the forestay. They painted both sails in dark hues to blend into the night's darkness.

Carlos, Roberto, and Zady devised five life jackets from the canvas remnants and some fragments of white foam.

The team members studying at the sports institute developed a training regimen. Their physical fitness program centered on enhancing three aptitudes: spinal muscle robustness for rowing, increased resilience against exhaustion, and tolerance to motion sickness.

To combat seasickness, they devised a series of exercises to desensitize the cochlea, the inner ear's balance organ. Through simple neck stretches and circular motions, they aimed to lessen its sensitivity to motion. The team also practiced an unconventional exercise employing a baseball bat. Holding the bat vertically on the ground, one person would bend forward and rest his forehead on the bat's knob, then they would walk in circles around the bat while maintaining contact. After completing five circles, they would reverse direction. This was a quite challenging endeavor since it was often hard to complete the first set of circles.

Raul constructed a rowing bench at his house in Víbora Park. The machine used rubber strips salvaged from motorcycle inner tubes to generate resistance. By simulating a rowing motion and pulling the rubber strips from a seated position, the men effectively strengthened the muscles essential for rowing.

Days later, Carlos built another piece of equipment simulating a seat and two oars, which replicated the rowing motion. It employed a pulley mechanism, ropes, and a weight load. The two brothers also borrowed some weight discs from a friend to intensify the workout.

With these innovations in place, the team began their training in two training locations, one nestled in El Calvario and the other in Víbora Park. The bicycle, as the primary means of transport, completed the training.

Yet not all tidings carried a hopeful tune.

In the early hours of March 13, 1993, a strong tropical depression hit the western region of Cuba. This meteorological phenomenon earned the moniker 'The Storm of the Century.' The house in El Calvario, where their covert boat was taking shape, endured its wrath but sustained substantial damage. A portion of its roof was lost, partially exposing the concealed attic. This misfortune wrought a setback in the vessel's construction, delaying progress and pushing back their intended departure date. Originally aimed for the end of April, their escape plan was now in limbo.

To make things worse, Ivan's involvement in the venture had waned. Despite his initial eagerness to join the expedition, Ivan had become increasingly distant during the last months. This unsettling development cast a shadow of concern among the crew members.

"Bro, has anyone seen Ivan?" Gerardo asked.

Roberto shook his head. "Not for days."

"Saw him a couple of weeks ago. He told me his wife was pregnant," Carlos said.

"Hmm... you think he got cold feet?" Gerardo asked again.

Carlos nodded, a hint of disappointment on his face. "Seems like it. In our last talk, he danced around the subject."

"Here's the plan," Roberto proposed. "Let's not push him or bring up the trip. If he's out, he'll step aside. We have Didier to replace him."

But drawbacks seemed to converge all at once. Sonia, Didier's mother, suspected something unusual concerning her son. She lived next door and was part of the family. It was impossible for her not to notice the group's secretive activities. One afternoon, she cornered Carlos and Gerardo.

"Listen carefully. If I find out Didier is part of this, I'll call the police!" Her eyes blazed with a fierce intensity, and her voice dripped with a menacing edge that made her a serious threat to the mission.

Sonia's reaction left the team in a state of bewilderment. It wouldn't be the first time a mother stood against her son's pursuit, fueled by fear he might perish at sea.

Sonia stood tall at nearly forty, with brown hair and light eyes. Despite the passage of time and the absence of the luxuries of beauty care that most Cuban women embrace, Sonia exuded the distinctive allure she possessed in her younger days. She was the typical mother bear, marked by strength and tempestuousness and willing to do anything to protect her child. At times, she exhibited aggression and dominance, while at other times, she displayed tenderness and affection, resulting in a mosaic of emotions that made her reactions highly unpredictable.

"No, Sonia, no. Didier isn't coming with us," Gerardo tried to calm her down, his voice cracking with tension.

Sonia looked at Gerardo, her gaze piercing and her tone authoritative. "Just keep my son out of it."

The two friends rushed to inform the others about the incident.

"So, what do we do now?" Raul asked in astonishment. "We gotta tell Didier to stay away from us."

Roberto let the news sink in, his mind searching for alternatives. "That's not good. I designed the raft for a crew of five. We gotta find a replacement before the month ends."

"I can't see how," Carlos mused, his tone heavy with doubt. "Finding someone like Didier won't be easy."

Carlos's words resonated as an undeniable truth. Didier possessed both physical prowess and the crew's trust, qualities vital for the mission's success.

Mid-April arrived, and everything was in place except for two crucial elements. First, the absence of the fifth member, a gap that still needed filling. Second, the development of an escape strategy, a carefully crafted plan encompassing not only the crew's actions but also the establishment of a ground-based support group. This auxiliary team would create a diversion scenario to veil the main crew's clandestine activities. They would also watch the surrounding areas and communicate through visual signals to ensure the expedition could reach the shore without being detected.

Aware of the concerns inevitably arising, Roberto took proactive steps. He engaged in a series of conversations with relatives and friends, their faces mirrors of skepticism and apprehension. To gain their trust, he had to persuade them that the likelihood of failure was minimal. Each interaction resembled a rigorous academic defense, but Roberto thoroughly addressed every doubt and query.

The path toward persuasion was riddled with complexities, especially with his mother, Carmen. She crafted new questions daily like delicate tapestries, each thread an inquiry seeking to unravel her son's understanding of the quest ahead. Yet, Roberto's counterarguments were a testament to his reservoir of knowledge gained through diligent study. With each passing day, the chasm of skepticism narrowed, replaced by a budding trust in Roberto's insights. His patient explanations wove a fabric of understanding, stitching together not only his relatives' confidence but also their gradual embrace of the audacious proposed scheme.

Around this time, Raul visited his cousin Gonzalez in Santa Fe, a coastal town eight miles to the west of the capital. Despite their close relationship, the cousins had not seen each other in recent months.

Engaged in the culmination of his English bachelor's degree, Gonzalez navigated the final year of his career. His aspirations echoed those of multitudes of Cuban youth who yearned for a future with both promise and purpose, extending beyond mere subsistence. However, within the limitations of the island's existence, such aspirations were constrained, held back by an ambiguous future.

Gonzalez's eyes lit up, his surprise palpable. "Long time no see, cousin!"

"Well, if I don't show up at your doorstep, you don't make your way to mine, either," Raul teased, their hug sealing their bond.

"Oh, come on, you know I'm on the last stretch, and the finals are upon me. So, how's life treating you?"

"Surviving, juggling my studies and work," Raul said, a weary smile on his lips. "And your folks? How are they?"

"They're okay. Sticking to their routine, same old."

Raul sighed deeply; his next words tinged with a touch of resignation. "Same old shit."

Raul's words evoked the somber reality affecting every Cuban. In a communist society, the future was a bleak canvas painted with misery, regardless of how vigorously one pursued education or toiled at one's job. The oppressive government maintained an iron grip, treating its citizens as mere livestock. It was a grueling cycle, a life sentence in which hard work was mandatory. Deviating from this norm risked the heavy hand of the law, threatening sentences of up to eight years in confinement.

As people reached retirement age, there were two unappealing choices: continue working if health allowed or retire to await the inevitable embrace of death at home. Setting aside funds for leisure or travel was non-existent since pursuing wealth was a forbidden fantasy.

A hint of mischief appeared on Raul's face. "Look, if you have nothing in mind, let's go for a walk on the beach."

"That's a tempting proposition. Let's go enjoy the view," Gonzalez said, mirroring Raul's grin.

They strolled, exchanging words and thoughts. Eventually, they paused at a vantage point with a breathtaking view of the coastline. Seated, facing the sea, they allowed their conversation to subside into a companionable silence, eyes locked on the distant horizon.

"I'm leaving," Raul whispered, ensuring their conversation remained private.

Gonzalez reacted, puzzled. "Already? We've just arrived!"

"I mean the country."

"What?"

"You heard right. I've had enough of this. I'm leaving... on a raft."

"On a raft? Are you crazy?" Concern laced Gonzalez's voice. "You have any idea how many people have died?"

"Crazy would be staying here. Listen, we'll make it," Raul's response hinted he wasn't embarking on this journey alone. "I've got some friends, and we've been planning this for almost two years."

Gonzalez was at a loss for words. "I... I don't know what to say. Just be careful. And speaking of leaving, I'm leaving too. There're some people working on a deal to buy a boat, and they want me to join them, but nothing's sure yet."

"Well, now it's my turn to tell you to be careful. If you get caught on a boat, you'll go to jail. For sure, it's a stolen boat," Raul said, reminding his cousin most boats in Cuba are owned by the government or government-affiliated fishing cooperatives. "And those boats might be faster, but they're not necessarily safer."

"Oh, come on! Are you telling me a raft would be safer than a boat?" Gonzalez's incredulity was clear.

"I'm just saying... those boats' engines are too old and lacking maintenance. Many have altered parts. If the engine fails in the middle of the sea, the Gulf Stream's currents can easily capsize the boat. A raft, on the other hand, stays afloat."

Raul's explanation left Gonzalez deep in thought.

The conversation had instilled a notion in both men's minds. Without explicit proposals, Raul sensed the potential for Gonzalez to become the fifth crew member.

That night, Gonzalez tossed and turned, unable to fall asleep. He grappled with his cousin's warnings about the dangers of fleeing on a motorboat. After extensive contemplation, he made a resolute decision. The following day, he would make it his mission to find Rita, the clairvoyant.

Rita was renowned across Cuba for her uncanny accuracy in predicting events. She was tall and robust, with a tanned complexion and short, black hair. Her warm brown eyes exuded a gentle reassurance. Well into her third age, her premeditated motions matched her serene demeanor. Rita's exceptionalism extended beyond her spiritual gifts, as she declined to accept payment for her consultations. She counted on presents and humble donations without ever requesting them. Her genuineness attracted an abundance of individuals.

The clock struck ten. The bus from Santa Fe pulled over at the bustling intersection of San Rafael and Infanta streets in Havana. Gonzalez stepped off the bus with a determined stride and made his way toward a decrepit building on 818

Concordia Street, a few blocks away. Inside the building's weathered interior, he navigated a narrow corridor ending in a flight of stairs leading to the second floor - the location of Rita's apartment – and softly knocked on the door.

"Coming!" came Rita's response from behind the door.

As the door creaked open, the hinges squeaked, and the lady's face came into view.

"Hello, Rita! How have you been?"

With a welcoming gesture, she invited Gonzalez into her apartment. "Dealing with the ailments that come with old age. And what about you? It's been quite a while since I last saw you."

The young man stepped into the unassuming dining room. A clear glass cup holding water and a small bouquet of sunflowers in a simple white vase adorned the refrigerator. The room also hosted a diminutive metal replica of the miraculous Saint Lazarus. Its size didn't surpass five inches in height. It was her shrine, a testament to her deep spiritual convictions and modesty.

"I was in the neighborhood and thought I'd drop by to say hello," the young man said.

"Is that so?" Rita turned her eyes toward him. A maternal smile touched her lips, yet her expression held a hint of skepticism. "Oh, Gonzalez, young folks nowadays don't pay visits to old ones just for pleasantries. So, tell me, what brings you here?"

The young man hesitated briefly before speaking. "I'm planning to leave the country... and I need your guidance," he said, his confession like a whisper.

Rita's face softened. With serene composure, she gestured for Gonzalez to sit at a small table nestled in a corner of the room. "I'm truly glad you came to see me. Please sit down. You must relax."

With cautious movements, the young man lowered himself onto the chair. His elbows found a resting place on the table as his fingers intertwined in a blend of anxiety and curiosity. His gaze was fixed on Rita, observing her every move. Rita retrieved a well-worn set of tarot cards from one of the kitchen drawers.

She settled onto the chair opposite him, placing the deck of cards on the table. Her hands cradled the stack of cards, fingers interlaced reverently as her eyes closed in a silent invocation.

After a moment of connection with something beyond sight, she began shuffling the deck. She took her time. There was a magic dance between her hands and the deck of cards. She ceased and positioned the cards on the table.

"Split it into three and choose one," Rita instructed gently. The young man complied, splitting the deck into three portions and then selecting one.

The lady collected the three portions, placing the chosen one on top. Delicately, she drew the cards, each placement following a precise sequence.

"These letters show me two sea journeys heading in the same direction." Rita's initial words sent shivers down Gonzalez's spine.

"I never mentioned two groups to her... how could she possibly know that?" he thought.

"I see two distinct groups here. One, larger, too many people," she said, her words enigmatic. "Hmm! They will not reach their destination. They shall encounter opposing forces leading them astray and, eventually, back to their origin."

While Gonzalez listened to Rita's predictions, his cousin's warning echoed in his mind. "Those boats' engines are too old and lack maintenance."

"The other group, about five people, will have assistance, but that's because they've earned it with preparation and sacrifice. They will arrive at their destination."

Then, her gaze fixed on Gonzalez's eyes, she leaned forward and, in a soft yet enigmatic tone, imparted her advice. "If you cherish your behind, my dear, avoid the larger group. Go with the smaller one."

Both shared a laugh, a testament to Rita's sage counsel and her ability to infuse even the most serious matters with a touch of humor, leaving Gonzalez feeling both heartened and at ease.

"Do you have any other concerns?" she asked.

"No, I think you've already helped me a lot. Thank you, Rita."

With the cards gathered and a final prayer of gratitude, the session concluded. As Gonzalez made his way down the stairs, he turned back and waved farewell. Rita returned the gesture with a warm smile.

"Best of luck! And tell your friends to come see me!"

In the same week, Raul visited his cousin once more. After the customary pleasantries and a brief exchange, Raul cut to the chase. "Any progress on your plans?"

"I don't know, man. Your words got me thinking about that journey, and it's quite a risk."

"Listen, here's the deal," Raul paused briefly. "We're looking for a helmsman. Would you like to come with us?"

"Absolutely, but...?" Gonzalez's excitement quickly gave way to hesitation in his tone.

Raul picked up on his cousin's anxiety, even though he hadn't expressed his fear. "These guys are solid. Just wait 'til you meet them. Let me speak to them first, and I'll get you in."

"Alright, keep me posted. Oh, by the way, you know Rita, the card reader?"

"Of course, who doesn't? She's quite a character."

With an air of mystery in his voice, Gonzalez shared his encounter with the wise lady in detail. "And you won't believe it, but she asked me to bring the group for a reading."

"Man, I've got chills. I haven't told you yet... but with you, we're already five."

Later that day, Raul convened a meeting with his friends at Carmen's house in El Calvario.

"I believe I've found the man we needed." Raul narrated his conversation with his cousin, outlining Gonzalez's qualifications in detail, including his muscular build, proximity to the coastline, and fluency in English.

"Someone familiar with the sea, and he can also serve as an interpreter. He seems to be the guy," Carlos said.

"Great! Bring him over so we can all meet. It will also be a chance to give him some guidance on preparing for the trip," Roberto said, proposing a date for the meeting.

A few days later, the quintet convened in Carmen's house. Gerardo was the earliest arrival, and he joined the siblings already working on the project. An inflated inner tube rested against the wall, and a stack of empty rice sacks waited on the floor. The brothers were slicing the sacks into one-foot-wide strips with a pair of scissors. Precision guided their hands as they then meticulously sewed the strips together, forming an ever-extending tapestry of fabric.

As they added new pieces, they coiled the elongating fabric around itself. Then came the moment of assembly as they wound the fabric around the inflated tube, ensuring the strips enveloped the tube in a protective embrace. After they were done with the first tube, they unwrapped it and rolled the sack strip back. This way, they calculated the length of material needed to cover the entire tube. It was the first of four equivalent scrolls. For the fifth scroll, destined for the raft's bow, they needed a tapestry twice as long.

This wrapping would serve as a safeguard, a protective layer for the airlock inner tubes. It would be their armor against the potential abrasions inflicted by the raft's wooden frame and any trash floating at sea. The tales of previous voyages whispered in their ears, cautionary reminders of how errant debris had punctured other mariners' vessels, imperiling their lives. Each stitch, each piece of rice sack, was an investment in their future, a calculated defense against the unpredictable forces awaiting them on the open sea.

An hour elapsed until Raul and his cousin, Gonzalez, made their appearance. "What's up? From what I see, you didn't wait for us," Raul said, his hand reaching out for his friend's grasp. "This is Gonzalez, my cousin."

With an air of camaraderie, the rest of the crew warmly welcomed their fresh addition. After formal introductions and the exchange of hearty handshakes, Raul guided Gonzalez to the attic space. "Come with me. I want you to meet Esperanza."

"Esperanza? You never mentioned there was a woman."

Raul's lips curved into a knowing grin. "There she is."

Gonzalez walked around the craft, his eyes traveling the vessel's contours in sheer astonishment. "Damn! I pictured a raft, but this... this is like a galleon."

Moments later, the pair returned to the group. Gonzalez shared a concise version of his earlier plans to escape on a boat. He then explained how Raul's intervention and the clairvoyant's revelations had stirred a drastic change in his trajectory.

"Great! With you here, our team is now complete," Roberto said, his tone echoing satisfaction.

Later, Gerardo, recognized for his eloquent speaking, updated Gonzalez on all the endeavors accomplished up to that point. Meanwhile, the rest of the team continued with their meticulous work.

The sun had already traversed the morning into noon.

"One thing worries me," Gonzalez said just as he was about to leave. "It's about school. Exams are done, but now, I'm supposed to attend a military concentration camp. It's only for two weeks, but if I skip it, they'll come looking for me at my house."

A military concentration camp served as a temporary training school. The regime had instituted these facilities for those not actively enlisted in the armed forces. All male graduates had to partake in these training programs following their completion of higher education.

"Hmm, that's not good. We have a few days left, and we're far from ready," Carlos said, his voice tinged with urgency.

"Anyway, go to the training," Roberto said. "But stay in contact with Raul; he'll keep you informed."

Later, the cousins boarded a bus, taking line 68 to reach Raul's residence in Vibora Park. As the vehicle rolled along, the two young men engaged in conversation. Gonzalez conveyed his amazement at the team's impressive state of preparedness, singling out the raft for its colossal size and intricate design.

"Hey, if they let us reach the water, we'll get to the other side," Raul said, his words reflecting total confidence in his companions.

A few days passed, and the group, except for Gonzalez, who was away for military training, convened in Carmen's house once more to decide on the departure date. A 1993 twelve-page calendar lay on the table at the center of the reunion. Its first four pages were folded back, exposing the month of May with scribbled notes and reminders, a testament to its usefulness.

"I've been looking at the calendar," Roberto said, beginning his speech, "and we have two options in May: the first and the last week of the month. We'll have a new moon these weeks, meaning we won't see the moon, so the nights will be darker, and we'll have a better shot at getting away.

"Bro, I'd choose the first week. The closer we get to summer, the harder it will be to escape undetected," Gerardo said.

Aware that coastal surveillance increased during the summer, Carlos nodded in agreement. "You're right. But April is almost over, and we still haven't secured the food supplies for the journey."

Raul added, "And we also need the beach house for assembly. I'd pick the last week."

The raft needed to be dismantled for transport and then reassembled near the beach before departure.

"The last week sounds better to me," Roberto proposed. "We'll have a window of three possible days: Monday, Wednesday, or Friday, between 9:30 and 10:30 at night when everyone is likely glued to their televisions."

The young men chuckled at Roberto's comment, alluding to the Brazilian soap opera "Vale Todo" (Anything Goes), which aired on those weekdays. This show was quite popular in Cuba because of its comedic nature and the absence of political themes, which usually saturated the television schedule. Brazilian productions had seized the attention of the Cuban audience since the mid-1980s due to their disdain toward Marxist-Communist propaganda.

"Monday seems preferable," Roberto continued. "The guards might be worn out from partying the night before. We need the house rented for that day."

During his service, Roberto learned that the military command assigned Monday's guard to soldiers returning from their weekend pass. This was significant because many soldiers tended to party hard during their time off.

The last week of May was settled on as the date after a thorough analysis of the advantages and disadvantages.

"Hey, changing the subject," Raul interjected, "we should set aside a day to see Rita. She reads Tarot, and she's very good."

Roberto responded with a hint of skepticism. "I don't believe in that stuff, and we're running out of time."

"Well, I do believe there are stories about her predictions coming true," Raul said, his tone growing passionate. "You know what? I'm going to see Rita."

"Alright, alright, no need to get worked up," Roberto soothed his friend. "How about Tuesday?"

"That works for me, but we should all go," Raul insisted.

"Okay, we all go. Just tell your cousin to meet us there on Tuesday at 10. We'll meet here an hour before," Roberto said, sealing the decision.

And so it was. Just before 9:00 a.m. on Tuesday, Raul arrived at the house in El Calvario, where Carlos and Roberto were already waiting. About fifteen minutes later, Gerardo joined them. The four young individuals embarked on their journey to catch the Route 68 bus, which would transport them to their intended destination.

After about thirty minutes, the bus came to a stop, and the four men merged with the bustling crowd, resembling pirates boarding a Spanish ship. The scene was chaotic as people flooded onto the bus.

Around 10:00 a.m., the bus pulled into the Infanta and San Rafael stop. The team disembarked, and there they encountered Gonzalez, who had arrived shortly before them.

"Hello!" Gonzalez greeted.

"Hey!" the group responded, shaking hands with their newest team member.

"Have you been waiting long?" Raul asked.

"No, I just got here," Gonzalez replied. "Let's go; it's not far from here."

The young man guided his companions to Rita's modest apartment. Gonzalez and Raul, the most dedicated members of the group, strode ahead and led the way while the others followed closely. Upon reaching Rita's apartment, Gonzalez knocked on the door.

They heard Rita's voice from inside. "I'm coming!"

"Hello!" Gonzalez greeted as the door swung open.

"Hi, Gonzalez! Welcome back!" Rita responded with unabashed delight. "Come in, come in."

Gonzalez stepped into the apartment with a measure of assurance while the others exhibited more caution. They greeted the lady, who replied with a gracious smile.

"Don't be shy. Grab a chair and make yourself comfortable. I see you took my advice," Rita told Gonzalez as she closed the door.

"Yes! I brought the others," he said.

"Very well! Each of you will have an individual session. I'll ask the same questions to each one. Let's see what unfolds," Rita explained. "Gonzalez, take a seat at the table. The rest of you can wait here."

Roberto, perhaps because of his atheism, opted for a chair near the door, affording him a view of the lady's movements. Raul made himself comfortable in a chair next to Roberto. Carlos and Gerardo occupied chairs on the right side of the living room. Gonzalez took the same seat he had during his previous visit. Silence enveloped them as Rita's sandals produced a soft sound on the polished granite floor. Her body swayed rhythmically in perfect harmony with her steps, and like motion sensors, ten eyes closely tracked the seer's every movement.

Rita returned from the kitchen, shuffling her worn deck of tarot cards.

With a noticeable effort, the lady settled herself on the opposite side of the table, facing Gonzalez.

Then, Rita closed her eyes, clutched the tarot cards, and assumed a posture of prayer. The silent supplication lasted mere moments. Afterward, she extended both arms, placing the deck of cards in front of Gonzalez.

"The first question is, will you emerge from the ocean after you've entered it?" The seer asked, her hands concealing the cards. "I need you to concentrate and visualize the journey."

This query alluded to the peril many rafters faced in the ocean, often disappearing—either drowned or consumed by sharks.

Gonzalez closed his eyes, holding silence for a beat.

"Okay… I'm ready," he said.

"Cut the deck into three stacks and pick one," Rita said, moving her hands and revealing the cards once more.

Gonzalez followed her guidance and split the deck, pointing to the pack in the center.

The old woman's hands trembled as she picked up each pack and carefully rearranged them. She placed the chosen pack on top, then she revealed the cards on the table in a deliberate sequence, her soft murmur carrying on a dialogue with the cards.

Rita extended her right index finger, pointing at a particular card. "This card signifies 'yes,'" she said with a reassuring smile. The group's tense expressions relaxed upon hearing her words. Rita gathered the cards and shuffled them once more.

With a sudden shift in attention, she turned to Roberto with a soft smile on her lips. "I know you don't believe in this," she said, her gaze directed at him and her message resonating like a revelation across the room. She spoke in a gentle tone, trying not to make him feel uncomfortable. "But don't worry; all will be well."

Roberto, speechless, could not hide his surprise.

With no further explanation, Rita disengaged her chat with Roberto and refocused her gaze on Gonzalez. She guided him through the process, urging him to envision the outcome. "Let's visualize the end of this journey. Will you reach your destination, or will the authorities intercept you?"

Following the ritual, Gonzalez once again divided the cards and selected the middle group. Rita reclaimed the cards and proceeded with the ceremony. Her reaction was noticeable, a mixture of surprise and dissatisfaction gracing her countenance.

Gonzalez, startled, leaned forward, inquiring with urgency, "What is it?"

Rita offered clarification. "This card signifies 'the other shore,' your destination. However, the card representing authority appeared before it."

She explained the sequence suggested interception by authorities. "This card must appear to the others as well because you all are traveling together. But this outcome depends on the answer to the first question."

"And what if the answer to the first question is 'no'?" Raul asked, his voice hesitant as if he wasn't sure he wanted to know the answer.

"Then that person needs a 'cleansing session' before coming back to repeat the session. If the answer remains 'no,' my advice is not to embark because he will not make it."

As the conversation continued, the group's apprehension became palpable, and the prospect of negative predictions weighed heavily on them. Even Roberto, despite his skepticism, understood the psychological impact.

Rita continued her divination by shuffling the cards for the third question. She then instructed Gonzalez, "We need to know whether those who intercept you are Cuban or American authorities. Visualize that moment when you see the ship approaching."

With her cards placed before him, the process began anew. Gonzalez briefly closed his eyes, contemplating the question. He then divided the cards into three stacks and, this time, chose the pack on the right.

As Rita conducted her ritual, turning the cards with deliberate care, a mixture of tension and anticipation filled the room. When the seer's delighted exclamation broke the silence, a glimmer of hope appeared in Gonzalez's eyes. "It won't be the Cuban guards."

"No?!" he asked.

"This card signifies a foreigner," Rita said with a gentle smile. A wave of relief swept over the group.

Rita's conclusion sparked jubilation among the young crowd, especially Gonzalez and Raul since they knew of cases where Rita's predictions were fulfilled with extreme accuracy. With each member of the group, Rita repeated the ritual, and remarkably, the key cards maintained their consistent positions. This experience solidified the bond of trust among the prospective expedition members.

For Carlos and Roberto, the visit to Rita's house was a unique experience. The session was unlike anything they had ever witnessed before.

"Ma'am, how much do we owe you?" Roberto asked as the group expressed their gratitude to Rita for her invaluable guidance.

"Nothing! My faith doesn't allow me to charge for my services," she said with her customary maternal smile. "If people wish and are able, they offer something."

Pooling their resources, the group gathered twenty pesos, the equivalent of two days' worth of a doctor's salary, and presented them to the seer.

"Thank you very much. You know where to find me if you need me. Ah, I almost forgot..." Rita halted the young men on their way to the door, "When you get to Miami, go to Saint Lazarus' church in Hialeah and offer a prayer of gratitude. Particularly you, Gerardo, as he was very kind to you when you were in your mother's womb."

Goosebumps prickled Gerardo's arms as he remembered his mother's stories of the pain and struggle she endured during his birth.

"And you..." Rita turned to Roberto, "I see you surrounded by papers. You'll be working with documents. I can't discern the exact nature of the work, but it will bring you financial stability. So, you guys," she advised the others, "don't stray too far from him."

With newfound optimism, the five men bid farewell to Rita. The encounter had a profound impact on Roberto. It shook the foundations of the atheist-materialist philosophy instilled in him for years at school.

Throughout that week, Raul and Roberto scoured the eastern Havana beaches for an appropriate house to lease near the seashore. Despite their efforts, their initial trip turned out to be fruitless. Even with local residents' input, it was in vain.

The following week, Roberto teamed up with his mother, Carmen, to continue the search. She had some friends working at the beach. Through her friends' connections, they eventually discovered a modest house available for rent close to Boca Ciega Beach. After negotiations with the landlord, a rental arrangement was established at a rate of 200 pesos per day. However, the landlord did not provide any form of assurance or security for the agreement.

Time slipped away rapidly amid mounting anxiety at Carmen's house.

Roberto returned home one afternoon, the sound of his footsteps echoing through the silent house as he made his way up to the attic. An unexpected sight awaited him: his brother, Carlos, sat upon the raft, positioned where he would eventually sit as the team's front rower and holding the oars. He stared at the back of the raft, lost in contemplation of the unknown future.

"Have you told Tamara?" Roberto asked.

Carlos's response sounded more like a command. "No."

There was a long pause as his gaze dropped. "I don't have the stomach. Besides, I'm afraid she might call the police."

"What about your boy? How long until you see him again?" Roberto asked further. He understood his brother's impulsive nature and wanted to make sure he was fully aware of the impending suffering his departure would cause.

Carlos nodded, a mixture of confirmation and sorrow. "Can't stop thinking about it, but I don't have a choice. Can't even buy baby milk in this wretched country. At least I could send him money from Miami."

Roberto felt a deep ache for his brother and his young son, who had just learned to say "Dad." Little Juan Carlos was poised to become another innocent casualty of a human tragedy before his second birthday. The separation of families remains one of the most tragic consequences of communist regimes.

Roberto settled in a corner of the rustic, unfinished structure in silence. He shared his brother's anguish, and for a time, they both lingered there, words unnecessary amid their shared melancholy.

That evening, Roberto wrestled with restlessness. The nearing departure date cast a weighty emotional load on his shoulders. To unburden himself, he sought solace in a walk. His girlfriend joined him. They walked together along

Havana's Malecon, a famed seaside promenade frequented by tourists, strollers, and lovers. More than romantic partners, they were genuine friends, sharing their thoughts and secrets openly. Yet, on this walk, their camaraderie was tinged with an undercurrent of unease.

A maelstrom of emotions and contemplations churned relentlessly within Roberto's mind. As they strolled in a silence that felt heavy, Roberto's senses acted like vigilant radars. Every detail of their surroundings registered with heightened acuity. These moments could be his last memories of Havana, the weathered yet still captivating city. Roberto halted, directing his gaze out to the sea. Across the bay, he contemplated the legendary Morro Castle and its iconic lighthouse. Closing his eyes, he embraced the unmistakable scent of salt air clinging to the colonial structures. The symphony of ocean waves harmonized with the city's ambient sounds.

As nostalgia filled his soul, one thought resonated in his mind: "This could be the last time I walk this street."

In that bitter moment, Roberto's girlfriend sobbed, overwhelmed by her emotions. The impending departure of her beloved weighed heavily on her heart.

"Why the tears?" Roberto asked gently, though he already understood the source of her distress.

The young woman's fingers clutched Roberto's shirt as tears streamed down her cheeks. "I don't want you to go!"

"Hey, please don't cry," Roberto implored, his voice laced with empathy. He reached out to console his girlfriend, wrapping his arms around her and attempting to soothe her pain. "We've discussed this, and you know I can't abandon them."

"How will I go on without you?" she asked, her words seeping through her tears, her face buried in the safety of Roberto's chest.

Wrapped in an embrace, they shared a heartbreaking silence. No words could assuage the pain they both felt. For Roberto, it was as if his world was collapsing around him. His lover was acutely aware of the crew's roles and responsibilities in their impending journey. She understood the gravity of Roberto's task as the expedition's navigator, arguably the most crucial role.

At sea, devoid of familiar landmarks like buildings or trees, navigation relies on compasses and stars. The vast ocean is a canvas of two primary hues: blue by day and black by night. Maintaining an accurate course demands precision; even a few degrees of deviation could lead the expedition to a fatal destination.

Sunday, May 23, 1993, arrived as the scheduled day to secure the house rental. The team gathered in two separate groups, with Raul and Gonzalez forming the first, while the second comprised Roberto, his girlfriend, and his cousin Yeney.

They met the house owner as noon approached. Roberto took the lead in the conversation. "Good morning, ma'am! How are you?"

"Very well, my son. Thank you!"

"We'd like to rent the house... for two days."

"Alright, but you'll have to wait until the current occupants leave," she said, referring to the present occupants of the house. "They are waiting for someone to pick them up."

Roberto assured her, expressing his understanding. "That's fine, no rush. We'll be at the beach and will come back later."

As the day progressed, nearing five in the afternoon, Roberto called his mother. Communication was a challenge because of the antiquated telephone networks. Carmen informed Roberto that his cousin Reinaldo had borrowed a car from work. Reinaldo offered to help transport the heavier items to the beach house.

The raft had been disassembled the previous day to make its transportation manageable.

Reinaldo, accompanied by Lazaro, a family friend, arrived around six o'clock to load the cargo. They did this quietly through the back door. It was too risky to use the front door because it led to the main street, right next to a bus stop. However, the back door's proximity to a military counterintelligence officer's house posed another challenge. They had encountered no issues with the officer so far, but caution was essential.

As they returned from their second trip to the car, the officer emerged from her house and sat on her front porch. Reinaldo and Lazaro greeted her, receiving greetings in return. Subsequently, the men retreated to Carmen's house, waiting for the neighbor to go back inside. More than half an hour elapsed, yet the woman remained outside.

With time slipping away, the group could no longer afford to wait. They decided to take the risk and continued moving the cargo to the car, assisted by Ramon. Their actions were carried out with a carefully simulated nonchalance as if the task were of little significance. However, their efforts were disrupted by the nosy neighbor.

"What are you doing with those boards?" the officer asked boldly.

Reinaldo's quick response appeased the neighbor. "I'm going to fix my house's roof. It has many leaks since the storm."

The recent storm had damaged many homes in the neighborhood. The shortage of building materials had resulted in most damaged roofs remaining unrepaired.

Although they diverted the officer's attention for the moment, they knew she wouldn't give up easily. In anticipation of her persistence, they started the car's engine and circled the block before parking in front of the house, right along the main street.

Around 7:00 p.m., Didier arrived on his bicycle, panting as he delivered the distressing news.

"The beach is on fire!" he told his father.

"What?!" Ramon asked. His concern was palpable.

"I spent the night fishing with some friends. Border patrols searched our tent twice. They even inspected our fishing lines to verify if we had real bait," Didier said, his voice agitated, still short of breath. "Cops were everywhere!"

Ramon hurried to Carmen in the kitchen and shared the unsettling update with her.

"Maybe we should just get rid of all this," Ramon suggested urgently. "We can tell the boys the police stopped us on the road and confiscated everything."

"No, Ramon, I can't do that," Carmen asserted with unwavering determination. "My children put their trust in me. I can't let them down. I know their lives are at risk. Tomorrow, I might regret this decision, but right now, I'm praying to God and the Virgin Mary. I have faith they'll make it there safely."

Finally, Ramon conceded to proceed as planned. Amid the watchful eyes of the neighbors, they discreetly completed loading the raft on the vehicle. Then, the two young men with the cargo departed for the beach.

The mast, sails, and boom were too cumbersome to fit into the car and were left behind. The rudder, four oars, and some inner tubes also remained in El Calvario. These components could raise suspicion if Reinaldo and Lazaro came across law enforcement during their voyage.

As the night descended, tension grew among the waiting team on the beach.

"Have they been caught? Has the car broken down?" they asked each other as their anxiety built with every passing hour.

At last, the long-awaited car arrived. The sound of its engine was a welcome relief to the group's frayed nerves. The vehicle pulled up in front of the small beach house. Reinaldo stepped out and approached Roberto.

"Seriously? Why are they still here?" Reinaldo asked, surprised to see the house's occupants had not gone yet.

"These people! They were supposed to leave around noon," Roberto said, his voice filled with frustration. "They're packed and ready to go but still waiting for a ride."

"Will their delay mess up our plans?" Roberto's concerned thoughts echoed in his mind.

It was past 8:30 p.m. when the troublesome occupants finally departed the premises. Roberto paid the owner 400 Cuban pesos for a two-day rental, double the monthly salary of a professional technician. The young man and his team moved into the house with a sense of urgency, with no time to spare for cleaning. Swiftly, they transferred all their bags and equipment into the building.

As the night advanced toward 11:00 p.m., the car retraced its route back to El Calvario. Along for the ride were Roberto, his girlfriend, and Yeney.

That night, Raul and his cousin took up residence in the house, transferring the cargo to the largest room. Afterward, Raul fetched a bottle of rum, and the two men ventured out for a walk on the beach. Their aim was to gain insights into the nocturnal activities of the border guards.

As they reached the shoreline, the makeshift patrol split, with Gonzalez heading east and Raul heading west. The surveillance team would dispatch an advance squad to retrace the same path the next night. They hadn't ventured far from each other when Raul stumbled upon a pair of border guards sitting on the sand. The darkness was so profound that Raul nearly stepped on one of them.

"Oh, shit! You scared the heck out of me," Raul said, a profuse laugh filling the air.

"Sorry about that," they chuckled.

"How are you guys doing?" Raul asked.

With inherent Cuban warmth, Raul invited the guards to share a drink. After all, he, too, served in the military and empathized with these soldiers. He understood these young men would rather be anywhere but here.

"We're doing alright; just hanging in there," they responded.

Sitting down on the sand, Raul engaged in conversation with them while Gonzalez observed from a concealed distance.

"Have you seen a group of guys in a camping tent?" Raul asked to justify his presence. Given that camping on the beach late at night is a popular activity for youth, it was a safe guess.

"We noticed some people camping over there," one soldier said, pointing eastward toward Guanabo.

"I remember my years of service. Hated being on watch duty," Raul sympathized.

The soldier nodded in agreement. "Tell me about it."

"Imagine being out all night, rain or shine," Raul continued.

"Well, we have a house to rest in, but someone always stays out. Four of us cover from the Wooden Bridge to Guanabo's roundabout."

"Wow! That's more than half a mile. It sounds tedious... especially when it rains," Raul acknowledged as he stood up and brushed sand from his shorts. "I'm gonna keep going... see if I can find my friends."

As he walked away, one soldier called out, "Hey! Thanks for the drink!"

Raul turned back and replied with a smile, "No problem, comrade."

The endless night seemed to stretch on forever as anxiety and insomnia chased sleep away.

The house in El Calvario stirred with a sense of anticipation the following day. It was Monday, May 24, 1993. Departure day. Early morning saw everyone rising with a determination etched across their faces. The air was thick with unspoken emotions as they worked, their actions speaking louder than words. No elaborate greetings were exchanged, just a quiet "good morning." An air of melancholy blanketed their expressions, mingled with a palpable tension.

Carlos had already returned from Tamara's house, where he had spent the previous day preparing for Rosa's arrival. She was Carlos's mother-in-law. Ironically, she was coming back from visiting her family in Miami.

"Check this out," Carlos said, turning to his brother and displaying a small flashlight keychain that Rosa had brought him.

"That's exactly what we need," Roberto said with a nod of approval.

By 10:00 a.m., everything was in place for their departure to the beach.

They organized themselves into smaller teams of two or three people to avoid drawing attention to themselves. Each group departed from the house at five-minute intervals. The first subgroup comprised Aunt Titi, her daughter Yeney, and Diany, Raul's girlfriend. The second subgroup included Carmen and her daughter Zady; they carried the four oars. Gerardo and Ramon left through the back door carrying the mainsail, a deflated inner tube, and the radio cassette player. Carlos and Roberto took their time, waiting for about ten more minutes before they finally left.

The farewell was brief but emotional. Their grandmothers, Cuca and Zoila, were present, along with Sonia and Roberto's girlfriend.

Grandmother Zoila, Carmen's mom, masked her pain with reprimands. "We shouldn't shed tears for those who don't cherish us and leave us behind!" In contrast, Grandma Cuca and Sonia seemed like oceans of tears.

"I know I won't see you again!" Grandma Cuca lamented inconsolably.

Following the loss of her only son, Grandma Cuca became excessively attached to her grandchildren, particularly Roberto, whose resemblance to his deceased father was striking.

"Don't say that. You'll see us soon..." Carlos and Roberto attempted to console her in vain, their words choking on their throats as their emotions overwhelmed them.

The brothers collected their packs and the mast, boom, and smaller sail.

Roberto's lover embraced him tightly, her body quivering with emotion. Despite her efforts, tears streamed down her flushed cheeks. Roberto felt a piece of himself slipping away, and his legs almost refused to move. He kissed and held his girlfriend close, his heart heavy, bearing an indescribable pain. He closed his eyes, the world around him fading as he took a deep breath before turning away. Words seemed futile at that moment. Deep in heartache, the brothers left the house and gently closed the door behind them.

The day proceeded like any other. People scoured the streets in search of food for the day. Some waited impatiently for public transportation. Laughter and chatter filled the sidewalks as individuals spun their daily struggles into jokes. However, amid the clamor of voices and the occasional roar of passing cars, the two brothers heard nothing. All they could hear were their grandmother's words, "I know I won't see you again," reverberating in their minds.

They halted and turned back at a street corner. Their gaze lingered on their home one last time. The walls, aged by a century of existence, stood like witnesses to the ceaseless march of time.

"Going fishing?" a neighbor asked, interrupting the brothers' thoughts.

"Eh...! Yeah, fishing," the brothers responded with a strained smile, continuing on their path.

As they walked, the two brothers felt as if the worn soles of their sneakers were gently brushing against the ground beneath them. Leaving their neighborhood meant leaving behind their past lives. An uncertain new future awaited them, full of sacrifices, aspirations, and dreams.

"I never thought I'd feel so attached to this old town," Roberto mused inwardly. "I'm going to miss you."

They reached the highway, where they caught up with the rest of the group and about a dozen people waiting for transportation, a common sight in the town. The group members intentionally kept a distance from one another. Meanwhile, Aunt Titi and her daughter, Yeney, had already found a ride in a car. Soon after, from her workplace, Carmen spotted a flatbed truck approaching. This company often sent construction materials to the beach area. Carmen moved swiftly away from the gathering and signaled to the driver by waving her arms.

Recognizing Carmen, the driver promptly stopped the truck. People who could climb the side panels rushed toward the vehicle like so many piranhas attacking their prey. The group members also blended in with the crowd, being careful not to show any sign of familiarity. It was crucial not to be identified as a distinct group.

On the way to the beach, a silence enveloped the group. Carlos, Roberto, and Gerardo observed each stretch of road left behind with nostalgia. These were the same roads they had traversed countless times on their bicycles, and now, they were saying farewell to this familiar landscape of memories.

As the truck rumbled along, passengers would signal their stop by tapping the cabin's roof. Gradually, everyone disembarked, leaving only the group onboard until they reached the beach. Once off the truck, they dispersed, each taking a different path toward the rented house. Some circled the block to ensure they weren't being followed, and in pairs or small groups, they entered the house.

"How's everything?" Roberto asked his two friends.

"All good!" Raul responded.

Gonzalez's response came with a complaint. "Last night was awful... those itchy mattresses and swarms of mosquitoes."

"Alright, let's get to work. We have a lot to do," Roberto said, a sense of urgency in his voice.

Without delay, the five men occupied the two rooms. Some focused on assembling the raft, while others used a modified refrigerator motor as an improvised air compressor to inflate the tubes. Meanwhile, the women took over the kitchen. While making lunch, they kept bringing drinks to keep the crew hydrated.

Around midday, Mr. Perez and Estela, Gerardo's parents, arrived. They brought guava candy and peanut nougat bars, purchased coincidentally that morning from a street vendor. This, along with a few boiled eggs and sugared water, would form the essence of their diet.

After a brief pause for lunch, the clock ticked past 2:00 p.m., when Roberto suddenly realized the harpoon, a packet of sugar, and a few other essential items were missing.

"We need someone to go back."

"I think we'll be fine," Gerardo said. "We have enough sugar, and with the bottle of diesel, the harpoon might not be necessary."

"We can't leave the harpoon. If a shark gets too close, then what?" Roberto asked, emphasizing the importance of this last line of defense against sharks in case the diesel failed.

"I'm going," Carmen said. "My company's trucks pass through here frequently. I can make the trip quickly."

"I'll go with you," Zady, Carmen's daughter, volunteered.

They promptly prepared to leave while the rest of the group remained in the house.

As the afternoon progressed, the weight of the impending departure became more palpable.

"Check on Gerardo," Carlos asked his brother.

Roberto entered the room where his friend was. Gerardo sat in a corner of the bed, his chin resting on his hands and his eyes cast downward. Roberto stood before his friend, leaning against the wall and remaining silent.

After a moment, Gerardo looked up at Roberto, his eyes glistening with tears. "You need to tell my dad to leave because I... I just can't handle it," he implored, his voice cracking with emotion.

"It's okay. I'll talk to him," Roberto assured, trying to offer comfort.

Roberto made his way to the kitchen, where Mr. Perez stood in a corner, attempting to contain his own tears.

Mr. Perez, weathered by his 60 years, was a humble and diligent man marked by an amiable and willing disposition.

Like his wife, he held an unwavering love for Gerardo, their only son.

"Everything will be fine," the young man reassured his friend's father.

"I can't help it," Mr. Perez sobbed. "Gerardo is my only son, and the thought of losing him terrifies me."

Roberto understood Mr. Perez's fear. According to statistics heard on Radio Martí, only one out of every four rafters who jumps into the sea reaches the United States. This was the harsh reality that weighed heavily on their minds.

After a brief pause, Roberto spoke up.

"If you truly want to help us, you should go home," Roberto asked the older man, his voice trembling with pain.

Those words were undoubtedly difficult for Mr. Perez to hear. However, he comprehended the necessity. Mr. Perez made his way to say goodbye to Gerardo.

"Son, please take care of yourself," the father entreated, his voice fragile and quivering. His gaze remained focused on Gerardo's worn tennis shoes, a means of concealing the overwhelming grief in his eyes.

Father and son embraced heartily, their bodies trembling as unspoken emotions filled the air. Mr. Perez's tears dampened Gerardo's left shoulder. The father kissed his son and then left.

Roberto accompanied his friend's father to Main Street, and there, they exchanged farewells. With great sorrow, the young man watched Mr. Perez as he walked his way to the bus stop, his tears discreetly wiped away. Overwhelmed by grief, Roberto headed toward the beach instead of returning to the house. He thought about his brother, Carlos. The idea of him kissing his little son goodbye broke Roberto's heart.

Overcome by a mix of emotions, Roberto found solace in solitude. The armor of detachment he had worn for so long suddenly felt suffocating, urging him to break free.

He strode along the shoreline, the gray sky mirroring his somber mood. The brisk wind slapped his face, a tangible echo of his inner turbulence. The sea unleashed its anger, its waves crashing defiantly beyond the ordinary limits imposed by the sand. A wintry aspect added a tone of sadness to the deserted beach.

Seeking solace, Roberto found a companion in a rugged coconut tree, its weathered, twisted trunk a silent confidant. He stood there, lost in his thoughts, his hand tracing the tree's contours, connecting with the strength rooted in the earth. He contemplated the coastal landscape, the witness of many memories.

"Will I see this beach again? Or my family? What if we don't make it? What will happen to them?" As he thought about his life ahead, tears welled in his eyes and spilled down his face.

Facing the expanse of the sea, Roberto settled onto the sand, his back finding support against the coconut tree's embrace. His arms wrapped around his knees, drawing them close to his chest. The chill of the wind matched the winter in his heart.

"Of course, we'll make it! We're gonna make it, and one day, I will come back! Yes, I will!" Roberto whispered to himself, wiping away the tears, reaffirming his resolve.

————⟪(—✝—)⟫————

As the sun's dim silhouette vanished behind the clouds on the horizon, the day sank into dusk. Back at the house, Carmen and Zady returned from El Calvario, bearing the recovered harpoon and other necessities.

Roberto's crewmates joined him on the beach. The wind gained momentum, whipping their hair, and the waves surged with increasing intensity. They gathered on the sandy shore, facing the growing darkness of the night, their eyes fixed on the escape route.

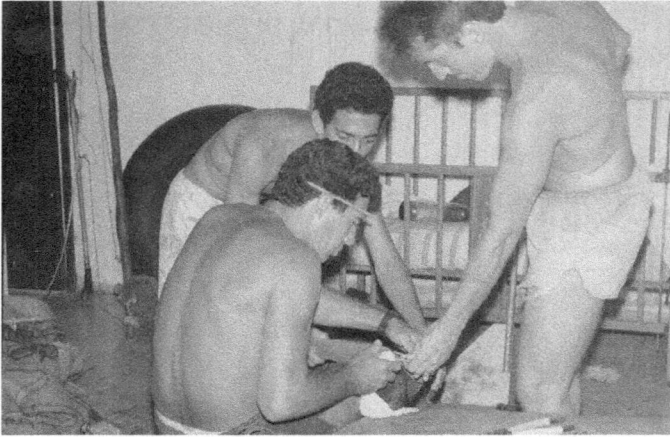

Carlos (at the front), Roberto, and Gerardo working in the house of El Calvario. On the floor (left corner), pieces of rice sacks. In the background, an inflated tube and the branch that would function as a boom.

Point on the beach where the group later escaped. Roberto walks towards the beach, holding high a two-liter bottle filled with water and sugar. To the right are Aunt Titi and Estela. In the background, a two-story building behind which the rented house is located. Photo taken by Raul a few hours.

4

THE DEPARTURE

Hardly has the first puff of smoke left the soldier's mouth when Aunt Titi speaks, her words tumbling out in a rush as if she has just remembered something critical.

"Guys, we're missing the soap opera!"

"Right! It's past 9:30!" Glancing at his wristwatch, the patrol leader concurs. He takes a quick second puff and passes the cigarette to his companions. "Let's find a TV."

The soldier refers to locating a house with a television they can watch from the sidewalk. Cubans often watch television at home with their windows open because of the heat and lack of air-conditioning. Fortunately, this would require the soldiers to walk away.

Despite being at the gates of the 21st century, Cuba remains stuck in the 1950s. They use black and white TVs, and almost half the households on the island don't have one. Like most electric appliances, televisions are deemed luxury items, and they are not sold to the public. Instead, citizens must earn the 'right to buy' such appliances through work appreciation. Each year, the government assigns one or two appliances per workplace, and the company's management decides who will receive the reward as job recognition. To participate, workers must be engaged in pro-state political activities. Furthermore, participants must have accumulated hundreds of hours of voluntary, unpaid labor. The winner receives an authorization certificate granting the employee permission to buy the described item, and he must present this authorization at the time of purchase.

Carmen catches on to her sister's secret plan.

"Guys, we should check at the Zone," she says. "They should have a television there."

The Zone is a management office responsible for sales and reservations in the beach area. It resembles a small hotel lobby and is just two blocks west of the rented house.

"No, no, we can't go to the Zone! An officer could see us," the group's leader rejects Carmen's idea.

The man's response does not surprise Carmen as she deliberately tries to push the soldiers away. Her sister and the others go along with the stunt and leave the porch, pretending they are going to the office. Unaware of any suspicious behavior, the guards continue their rounds toward the beach.

Ramon stays at the front gate and watches the soldiers walk toward the beach until they cross Main Street and disappear into the dark. Meanwhile, Zady and Diany, still shaken by the close call, remain frozen on the porch. But as they regain their composure, the two young women venture to the beach to watch where the guards are heading.

"Look, look! There's one," Zady whispers, pointing to a dark shape on the sand.

"Yes, he's crouching. Let's wait and see if he leaves," Diany says.

They have crossed Main Street and reached the sand, and the thick darkness prevents them from seeing beyond their hands. The headlights of a passing car driving down Main Street sweep across the beach, and the women's fears dissipate.

"Oh! It's just a log," they giggle with relief. They hurry back to the house to report that the coast is clear.

With a sudden jerk, the door swings open. Its hinges crack, catching the men's attention.

"The border guards are gone!" Ramon bursts in, his voice infused with urgency.

Startled, the young men exchange glances, momentarily jarred from their thoughts. They turn their attention to Ramon, their faces a mixture of surprise and anticipation.

"It's now or never!" Ramon's words cut through the room, and the crew members snap into action, reorienting themselves from their dazed state.

"Is the road clear?" Roberto asks, his voice charged with urgency.

"I don't know," Ramon replies, his hand still on the doorknob. "I'm going out to check. Be ready for the signal when it comes." With that, he slips out, leaving the door slightly ajar.

Ramon returns to the dark room. There, he briefs the five crew members on the situation outside. Although only a few minutes have passed since the soldiers' visit, it feels like an eternity to the men standing by inside the dwelling.

With the guards gone, Ramon exits the room and joins the support personnel gathered on the porch.

"The boys are ready," he says to the vigilance team. "They're just waiting for our signal."

"Okay, let's go then!" With two hand claps, Carmen hustles the group.

The members of the surveillance team hurry to take their predetermined positions. They will monitor the area and ensure the path to the beach is clear before the expedition team exits the house. Ramon and Zady act as an advance patrol. Holding hands, they pretend to be a couple as they head toward the shore. They follow the expedition's route to the water and then head west. They are prepared to strike up a conversation with the guards if they run into them.

Carmen stands at the intersection's north corner, watching Main Street, the most dangerous point on the movement to the coast. Main Street is lit up, albeit minimally. There is also the possibility of a casual encounter with a passing vehicle. About fifty meters from Carmen, Diany stands in front of the house, completing the chain to carry the signal to those inside the building. Aunt Titi and her daughter, Yeney, watch the southern intersection. Estela, half a block away from the house, is the connection between Aunt Titi and Diany.

The five men inside the house anxiously stand by, staring at the front door. With their backpacks on and flanking the raft, they wait for the door to open and to get the go signal, knowing that peeking outside is too risky. Their hearts race and breathing becomes labored as stress reaches an unbearable level.

It is 10:20 p.m. when the plan springs into action. Diany opens the door and signals the five men.

"Now!"

Roberto turns off the porch light, and the men push the raft through the door's narrow frames and out of the house with great difficulty. Esperanza, turned on her side, squeezes through the exit. As they push forward, they are careful not to damage the tubes with any wood splinters. Roberto presses the largest tube with his hands as it passes through the door. They must prevent the delicate airlock tubes from getting damaged at all costs as they rub against the rough wood.

However, time is of the essence. Although the house is dark, the only streetlight on the block shines brightly across the street. The first tire at the raft's bow is the biggest one. Its way through the narrow exit is difficult, like a baby passing out through the birth canal. The men force it out, but it takes the team almost thirty seconds to push the enormous tube through the door. That is too long. Fortunately, the other four tubes are smaller and offer less resistance.

Once Esperanza is on the porch, the five men take their positions on either side of the raft, holding it sideways. They lift her up and sprint down the street. The men's steps are short and unsteady under the raft's weight, making its transfer strenuous. They pass the porch's gate and reach the street. There is no sidewalk, so the camouflaged group moves swiftly and silently along the edge of the road, carrying their heavy companion. They follow the planned route, skirting the road from the house to Main Street and rushing across the lit avenue before disappearing into the darkness of the sandy beach.

They run toward Carmen, who signals them to stop from her vigilance spot. Diany, advancing parallel to the group, sees Carmen's signals and calls out.

"Stop, stop!"

The men come to a sudden halt, but they are already halfway there, and there is no turning back. They put Esperanza down and cover her with their bodies, forming a bulky shape on the desolate roadside. Diany ducks down behind them. In the dark, their collective motionless silhouette could be mistaken for a parked vehicle. Their quick reactions reveal it as a well-rehearsed drill.

A lone cyclist approaches down Main Street.

They have heard about escape attempts going wrong because of casual encounters like this. The group remains motionless while Carmen starts walking along the sidewalk to avoid attracting the cyclist's attention.

The man rides past Carmen, oblivious to the group's presence. She watches him until he disappears, and then she turns around and signals for the expedition to continue.

The young men get up, hoisting Esperanza aloft and picking up their hasty march, followed by Diany. They reach Main Street and quicken their pace. This is the most dangerous part of their route to the shore. Fortunately, the street is deserted, with only the sound of the whistling wind and crashing waves adding to the eeriness of the night. Carmen crosses Main Street and reaches the sand. Her silhouette fades into the blackness. She keeps watching as the group with the raft approaches.

"What the...?!" Fear grips the group, and they brace for the worst as an intense light illuminates the entire intersection.

A white beam pierces the dense darkness, lighting the beach ahead. For a moment, they think it is the border patrol's searchlight, but they don't stop.

Mounted on a truck, the government uses military anti-aircraft searchlights to watch the seashore at night. They randomly move this vehicle from place to place.

"Hurry up!" Roberto squeezes the reserves of breath from his lungs to make himself heard over the stormy din.

The race to reach the sand becomes almost frantic as they sprint with the heavy load. They don't know the source of the lights is a public bus with high beams coming in their direction from two blocks further south. The vehicle moves down the street where the house is located. It stops to drop a passenger off at the corner where Aunt Titi and her daughter stand. They realize the danger the light represents for the escaping group, and they act. While the bus driver talks to the man getting off, the woman and girl walk toward the vehicle, their shadows growing larger as they get closer. They stop a few meters from the bus, using their bodies to block the light beams from reaching down the street.

Their quick action returns darkness to the area, and courage rises within the fleeing group. The escape team crosses Main Street and ventures onto the sand.

Meanwhile, on the bus, the passenger says goodbye to the driver.

"Thanks, buddy. See you tomorrow."

"See ya," the conductor replies.

Aunt Titi and Yeney step aside, and the whole street lights up again. The vehicle closes its door and starts moving.

Fortunately, it turns right at the intersection and continues its route toward Guanabo Beach.

By now, the team is passing Carmen. Clutching her chest with both hands, she lets out a broken and trembling goodbye.

"Go with God!"

Aided by the last flash of light from the bus, Roberto looks at his mother's face as tears of emotion and pain run down Carmen's cheeks. The emotion a mother feels when she sees her children turned into men and challenge their destinies. The pain a mother suffers knowing this may be the last goodbye.

"Take... care," Roberto says, struggling to speak, his oxygen depleted after the demanding race from the house.

The group carrying the raft now trudges toward the shore. Their feet sink into the fine sand, which clings to their shoes, hindering their progress.

In the darkness, Carmen realizes her white shirt could give the team's presence away, and she drops to the sand, with Diany following suit. They watch as their loved ones run toward the unknown, and their silhouettes vanish into the night.

As the group advances, their feet sink deeper into the sand. The march becomes slower and more grueling, and the longing to reach the water turns to desperation. The exhaustion is extreme, and a couple fall to their knees just steps from the bubbling foam. Esperanza falls with them.

"Get up! Get up! We're almost there," they say as they encourage each other, pushing their bodies to their physical limits.

The last steps become a significant test of their willpower. Those who fell continue crawling, pressing forward with every ounce of strength they have left as they try to recover.

"Agh..." A grunting sound comes out from Gonzalez's throat. And the raft moves forward, its bow carving a path through the sand.

With the weight of the raft's stern against his chest, Gonzalez pushes the heavy vessel forward, defying his own limits. His friends don't miss the opportunity and join him. With one final push, they reach the shore, where the restless sea gives them a chilly reception.

The raft lands on the spumous surface, which cushions its impact. Scarcely have the young men gotten their feet wet when the first wave hits them waist high. The intense race and sudden contrast in temperature between their body heat and the cold water cause an intense desire to urinate, but they can't stop. They must keep going. However, their bladders cannot wait any longer, and the warm sensation of urine runs down their thighs. Carlos, Roberto, and Gonzalez push the raft into deeper water. They must get away from shore as soon as possible. Meanwhile, Raul and Gerardo return to retrieve the container hidden in the bushes.

The group struggles against the relentless waves, each crash throwing them backward as the raging sea refuses to be conquered. Although the water level barely reaches their waists, they are completely soaked. Raul and Gerardo rejoin the group, bringing the heavy container and placing it inside the boat. Roberto, the most agile of the team, takes the lead. He climbs on the raft first to set the front oars. The oars had been tied to the side rails so they would not fall during the march. Roberto unties the left oar, but the right oar gets entangled in its securing line. Carlos boards and sees his brother struggling with the tangled string. They have no time for this, so Carlos takes the right paddle and pulls with force. Its binding snaps. The brothers set the front oars in place, and Roberto moves to the center of the vessel, making room for his brother, who starts rowing. Esperanza advances slowly, and the three friends in the water keep pushing forward. If they stop, the wave will wash them ashore.

The water now reaches their chests. Gerardo climbs up and moves to accommodate the rear oars. Gonzalez ascends next and proceeds to secure the backpacks and the container with water and sugar and sets the rudder. Meanwhile, Raul keeps pushing the boat from below until he loses his footing, and the water engulfs him.

The last man tries to board the raft, but his water-filled backpack drags him back, hindering his efforts. He does not give up and attempts to climb up several times but in vain. Exhausted from fighting against his backpack's weight, Raul's arms give up. His hands cling to the raft's lateral rail, but his body is submerged.

Carlos speeds up the rhythm of his arms, knowing the front oars are the only means of propulsion until his friends set the rear oars. He sees Raul struggling, but he cannot abandon his oars. If he stops rowing, the relentless waves will drag the expedition toward the shore. Nor can he call out to his friends. A voice on the deserted beach would sound like an alarm. Facing the stern, Gonzalez secures the heavy container filled with their main food supply, ensuring it doesn't fall into the dark waters. Gerardo, closest to Raul, is setting the rear oars, unaware of his friend's predicament. Roberto is facing the bow, securing his and his brother's backpacks. He stops, glances around to assess the crew, and realizes Raul is missing. Roberto swiftly turns, searching for his friend and sees Raul's hands clinging to the structure right next to Gerardo.

By stroking his leg, Roberto alerts Gerardo, his voice low, almost like a whisper, but firm and urgent, "Help that man!"

They had carefully planned the escape to avoid talking during its execution. However, Raul is in danger, and Roberto has no choice but to break the silence.

Gerardo leans over the rail and grabs Raul by his shirt's collar. With Gerardo pulling him up, Raul makes one last attempt, hoisting himself over the boat's side rail.

Raul lies on the raft, panting heavily. He is exhausted, and his legs trail in the water. With a huge effort, he frees himself from the heavy backpack that almost drowned him. Gonzalez ties Raul's backpack next to him in the back of the raft.

Moments later, as he starts to recover, Raul regains his breath, pulls his feet out of the water, and slowly crawls to Gerardo's left by the rear oars.

The roaring sea continues to toss the small vessel around. Darkness shrouds everything, making the horizon disappear into the void, but their thirst for freedom prevails over adversity. The expedition leaves the shallow waters behind where the breaking waves had battered it mercilessly.

As the boat enters deeper waters, the waves, though bigger, no longer curl up on themselves. Roberto takes the first life jacket out of a backpack and puts it on. He needs to move around the shifting structure, and a crew member is more vulnerable to being thrown into the sea while changing position. After adjusting his homemade lifejacket, Roberto hands out the remaining four vests. He puts one on Carlos at the front oars and then Gerardo and Raul at the rear oars, so the rowers don't have to stop. Finally, he hands Gonzalez the last vest. Then, he returns to occupying his rowing position next to his brother.

"Tie on your safety ropes," Roberto whispers to the crew as he settles down on the front rowers' seat.

The safety rope is an essential tool for the crew as they navigate the treacherous waters of the Florida Straits. Each member carries a cord over three meters long. If he falls overboard, the safety rope will stop a man in the water from being dragged away by the strong current. However, the rope must not be too short; a short safety rope could be fatal. It must be just the right length to prevent a man from getting trapped underwater if the boat capsizes. They keep their safety cords rolled inside their pants' pockets to avoid getting entangled. Each man ties one line's end to his belt while securing the other end to the raft's rails.

During the two-year preparation for their risky endeavor, the crew learned that many rafters had lost their lives because of an accidental fall into the water. Sometimes, a wave capsizes a boat or throws a crew member out of a vessel. Often, rafters jump out to their deaths because of hallucinations caused by sunstroke, hunger, thirst, extreme exhaustion, and the desperate desire to see land. This explains why rescuers have found many empty rafts. If a man falls or jumps into the water, he encounters a current that drags him away from his boat. At the surface, the Gulf Stream has an average speed of five miles per hour. This is twice the walking speed of a healthy person. It is impossible for the already-weakened crew member to swim against this current. If an accident happens during the day, other travelers can mobilize to rescue the person in the water. Assuming the people on the boat are still in good physical and mental condition, they could divert their course and row toward the adrift person. During the night, however, the situation could be fatal.

Nights at sea can be awfully dark, especially if there is no moon. Darkness is almost absolute. In such conditions, if someone falls off a vessel with no safety line attached, the probability of being rescued diminishes greatly. Without visual clues, humans cannot pinpoint the direction that cries for help are coming from. Anyone who has looked for a cricket in the dark has experienced this human disability. The situation can turn to tragedy if there is no visual contact between the crew and the one in the water. Those remaining on board can hear the unfortunate person's despairing cries. Frantic, they scream back, but by the time they set their oars and start rowing, the person in the water could be over a hundred feet away. The crew will row blindly, trying to find the castaway, but they will hear the screams getting more and more distant, blending with the roars of an implacable ocean, which collects a heavy toll for human error.

When adrenaline runs out, and exhaustion wins, silence takes over. All the chaos turns into a horrifying stillness, a deaf serenity felt only in the presence of death. With time, the tragic experience grows into nightmares, and those muffled screams will remain engraved in the survivors' memory, echoing in their dreams for the rest of their days. This could explain why some Cuban rafters avoid talking about their experiences at sea.

The expedition continues. Their progress is slow but steady as they leave the beach behind. The distraction team is also left behind, a dedicated group of relatives and friends, including mothers, sisters, and loved ones. People who put themselves at risk by helping the fugitives to escape. They face the possibility of being arrested, fined, and subjected to the social marginalization imposed on those who disagree with the regime. They had risked becoming outcasts.

The easterly wind continues to pick up as they move further away from shore, pushing the raft westward. The waves are growing larger but less choppy because of the deeper water.

Gonzalez has already secured the backpacks with the provisions and the container of water mixed with sugar. He adjusts his life jacket and begins assembling the rudder. Because he is at the raft's stern, facing the bow, Gonzalez also plays the role of forward observer. The rest of the crew, facing the stern, continue rowing, their eyes scanning the shoreline and flanks, always vigilant for any signs of fishing boats. Fishermen working with the border guard have captured many rafters in coastal waters.

After having traveled a safe distance from the breaking waves, Gerardo and Raul stop rowing and prepare to set the two keels as planned on land. Meanwhile, Carlos and Roberto increase the frequency of their rowing to counteract the temporary pause of the rear pair.

"The keels...! We left them behind!" Gerardo's announcement sends a jolt through the young crew, and the two front oars drop still in the water.

"What?! We really need those keels."

Having studied sailing navigation and being the raft designer, Roberto understands the keels' critical importance for their safety.

Because of their length, the crew could not assemble the keels inside the house. Otherwise, the raft wouldn't have fit through the narrow door. They planned to tie the keels to the raft for their escape, but in the rush, they forgot them.

The keels were two pieces of wood, four feet high and one foot wide. Their bottom ends were narrowed, making them look like two inverted fins. The raft's design allowed for both keels to be set vertically, one on each side of the raft, just below the rear oars. Their purpose was crucial: to give the boat stability and prevent it from capsizing. In the high sea, small vessels can easily capsize because of a wave's impact or an improper maneuver with the sails. The keels also help the vessel navigate in a straight direction. In addition, the upper part of the keels would support the rear oars. The crew had set these oars on the side rails to get away from the beach quickly.

The crew remains silent, staring at the scattered lights coming from the coast.

"Bro, we can't go back," Gerardo says, breaking the silence.

"Of course not!" Roberto agrees. "We have to go on without them."

Again, the four oars slice through the water with synchronized movements, and the fragile boat restarts its slow march. Despite the relentless waves, the young crew is well-trained and determined, working together as one. However, the coastal current, fueled by strong winds, continues to carry the expedition westward, and in just one hour, they've drifted over two miles west from their departure point.

"That's the Marazul Hotel," Carlos says, recognizing their location. They are over a mile from shore but know the area well.

"We have to keep going!" They galvanize each other, the urgency in their voices belying the exhaustion in their limbs.

The situation becomes more dire by the minute. The currents continue to push them west, ever closer to the guarded beaches of Tarará.

Built in 1940 by Royal Sylvester Webster, Tarará had been a community for wealthy families. This exclusive neighborhood on the beaches of eastern Havana comprised some 400 residences, a yacht club/marina, a movie theater, shops, a public park, and a church. After the triumph of the Revolution, Castro confiscated these properties. Later, the government turned the town into a children's summer camp. Since the late 1980s, Tarará also housed many children affected by radioactivity caused by the Chernobyl thermonuclear disaster in Ukraine in 1986. Now, the government is preparing the area for foreign tourism, and the town has become a highly secure area with a large police presence. The Condesa River, known as the Tarará River, defines the city's western border. At the river's mouth, a border patrol unit equipped with radar, searchlights, and speedboats guards the area.

The men know Tarará is the most guarded stretch of the coast, and they know the risk of being detected. Gerardo worked there as a children's guide and observed the guards' routine for the last two years.

Despite the crew's best efforts, progress is slow, and they are still being pushed westward. Soon, they will be sailing off the coast of Tarará.

The youngsters prepare to get past the guarded area. All they can do is lower their profile by keeping close to sea level and stopping any movement if they see the searchlight's beam sweeping the horizon. The four oarsmen keep their eyes fixed on the coast, looking for the slightest sign revealing the presence of a searchlight. Meanwhile, Gonzalez watches the flanks and forwards to avoid being surprised by a fishing boat.

However, not everything is a drawback. The waves, which have been hindering the boat's movement, now help the expedition evade detection by the radar, but the possibility of the border guard using the searchlight represents a latent menace.

It is past midnight, and the weather doesn't change.

They have left Tarará behind, the area of coastline they consider the greatest danger. Apparently, the windy night has kept the fishermen ashore because there is not a single light in the dark sea.

During the following hours, the raft's trajectory did not vary. The currents drag the boat west while the crew's willpower, manifested in the relentless strokes of their four oars, forces the expedition further and further north. As the hours pass, they sail off the eastern Havana coastline, watching as Bacuranao, Alamar, Cojimar, and the rest shrink on the horizon.

"That's Camilo Cienfuegos' town," Carlos says. "Soon, we'll be in front of Havana."

"If we keep up this pace, dawn will find us right in front of Havana's port," Gerardo shares his concern.

"Why don't we set the sails? Wouldn't we move away faster?" Carlos asks his brother.

"Yeah! With this wind, we'd fly, but I'm afraid the radar would detect us," Roberto shares his caution.

"But if we don't set the sails now, the coast won't be out of sight by sunrise, and then, we'll be screwed," Raul says.

"You're right!" Roberto nods.

It's almost 4 a.m., and the expedition is about four miles from the shoreline. By this time, surveillance has usually decreased.

For a moment, Roberto hesitates, thinking about his friends' suggestions. He turns around and scans the sea in all directions.

"Okay, let's do it!"

They are running behind schedule. They had expected to lose sight of the coast before dawn, but the weather had slowed their progress and taken them off course.

Immediately, the inexperienced sailors pick up the oars and untie the mast. They had moored the long pole and sails on the raft's port side to make transferring the vessel to the beach easier. Despite the pitch-black night and their exhaustion from hours of rowing, the crew moves with a newfound energy. They have been longing for this moment to arrive.

"It is done," Raul says as he releases the last knot.

Carlos and Roberto prepare to bring the mast to its vertical position. They crawl to the boat's center and kneel on both sides of the base where the pole will rest.

The mast base has a hole at the top and a stainless-steel bearing at the bottom. The mast's lower end must pass through the hole and rest on the bearing, stabilizing it in an upright position while allowing it to rotate for greater control of the mainsail.

As they struggle to lift the heavy mast upright over the unsteady raft, Raul and Gerardo hold the two brothers from behind. Carlos and Roberto continuously try to insert the mast into the narrow hole, but the dense darkness and the raft's movement prevent them from achieving their goal.

"We'll have to use the flashlight," Roberto says.

"But we'll be exposed," Gerardo warns his friend.

"We'll bunch up and shield the light, so it won't be seen from shore," Roberto replies.

The team huddles together, forming a human dome around the base of the mast. Roberto takes a tiny flashlight out of his shirt pocket. He had carefully wrapped the mini lamp in a plastic bag so it wouldn't get wet. The man removes the wrapper and turns on the flashlight. Its white light shines, contrasting with the blind darkness surrounding the expedition. For an instant, they see each other's faces, but they must act quickly. Carlos raises the mast once again and, with Roberto guiding its lower end, finally inserts the pole into the narrow hole. The log slides through the hole until its tip penetrates the bearing's inner ring at the base's bottom.

"Finally!" The crew erupts in cheers, and the light is turned off.

Roberto wraps the flashlight in the plastic bag and tucks it back in his pocket.

They swiftly start setting the rigging system. Gerardo and Raul tie the two backstay lines to the raft's stern while Roberto takes the forestay line and crawls to the bow's right corner, releasing his safety cord as he advances. The navigator reaches the rail's end. The wooden frame holding the bow's inner tube extends another four feet out. He leans his body over the rails and stretches out toward the bow, very close to the water. Roberto is literally in a pushup position with his knees resting on the rails and his hands at the raft's edge. He now needs to tie the rope, but as he lowers his head, dizziness strikes, and Roberto clings onto the boat tightly to avoid falling into the water. An involuntary contraction from his stomach ascends through his esophagus to his throat. His stomach is empty, and he does not vomit, though he inevitably feels stomach fluid reaching his throat.

Roberto lies motionless for a moment as the discomfort passes quickly, leaving only a bitter taste in his mouth. He refreshes his face, rinses his mouth with seawater, and finishes tying the forestay line. Then, he slowly climbs back and returns to his post. There, he shakes his head, fixes his gaze on a distant light on the coast, and remains static for a moment. He takes a deep breath as the seasickness finally subsides.

Roberto rolls his safety line and puts it back into his pants pocket to avoid entanglement and interference with another crew member. Then, he gets up to help Carlos, who has already set the boom. The two brothers untie the mainsail.

With the boom stretching eight feet, the crew has rigged two lines at its furthest end to secure its position. They built it from a straight tree branch, just like the mast. The boom not only controls the mainsail but also shapes it by forming a 90-degree angle with the mast.

Raul tugs on the cord tied to a reinforced patch at the sail's outer end. This line slides through a pulley at the boom's end, causing the triangular sheet to fully unfurl. Unlike standard sailboats, the raft's mainsail opens by being pulled out instead of up. Once opened, the sail rotates to the west, driven by the wind. Its large canvas flaps like a flag.

Carlos and Roberto crawl to the bow to set up the jib, a smaller sail made of a triangular-shaped canvas six feet high by four wide at its lower part. Unlike the mainsail, the jig has no mast pole. Instead, the forestay acts as a jib's mast, and its boom is fixed to the sail's foot.

The jib's purpose is to maximize the wind's energy. Along with increasing the windward sails' area (the flank where the wind blows), the jib reduces the turbulence that forms behind the mainsail, which slows the vessel down.

The two brothers unfurl the jib and set it in the correct position, tying its two tensor lines before returning to their posts at the front rowers' seats. From there, Roberto guides Raul to adjust the mainsail orientation. Following his friend's instructions, Raul pulls the mainsail's boom toward himself, forming a 45-degree angle with the raft. The mainsail swells, and the raft, Esperanza, moves forward.

As dawn approaches, the wind intensity decreases, slowing the expedition down. At this pace, the coastline won't be out of sight before dawn, so the crew decides to paddle, desperate to get out of the guard's binoculars' reach. About twenty minutes later, Roberto assesses the oars and the sails' performance.

"The sails are working fine. I don't think it makes any sense to keep rowing. We're not going any faster." Roberto's oar comes to a stop, and the other oars stop, too.

"I agree," Raul says.

"If it were up to me, I'd keep rowing." Carlos shows his determination to press on.

"We'd better rest now. We might need to row hard tomorrow," Roberto tells his brother.

"And what about food?" Gonzalez asks, breaking his silence with a touch of humor.

"Hmm, you're right!" Gerardo says. "It's time to eat something."

Gerardo, who graduated as a veterinary technician two years ago, is the expedition's doctor and oversees the crew's eating schedule. His backpack contains a first-aid kit with seasickness medications, oral rehydration salts, adhesive bandages, and a needle and thread for wounds.

The crew retrieves the oars and secures them inside the raft. Gerardo pulls up a two-liter bottle from his backpack. He found the empty container a couple of months ago outside the Marazul Hotel. Evidently, a tourist from abroad had discarded the bottle as Cuban markets did not offer these soft drinks for sale to the public. Instead of its original Cola drink, the bottle now contains a mixture of water, sugar, lemon juice, honey, and salt. Gerardo shakes the plastic jar and removes its cap. He takes a sip and passes the jug to Raul as an expression of distaste appears on his face.

Raul grabs the bottle and drinks a mouthful before passing it to Carlos.

"Damn! It tastes like syrup," he says.

"Man... too much sugar," Carlos says, directing a questioning look toward Roberto and Gerardo, the ones who prepared the cloying mixture.

"It doesn't matter, mate. The important thing is to pour something inside," Gonzalez shows off his appetite.

The crew shares some laughs, letting out some of the stress they've been holding in since their escape.

"It's true. This stuff is too strong to swallow," Roberto says, admitting they had, indeed, used too much sugar in the mixture.

"That's the whole idea, bro," Gerardo says. "We need lots of calories to stay in shape."

They sail about five miles from the coast in front of 'La Playa del Chivo' (Goat Beach), a coastal strip between Camilo Cienfuegos's city and the imposing El Morro castle. Defying the elements, the fortress rises high above a large rocky formation, reaching the height of a fifteen-story building. On its tower's top sits its legendary lighthouse.

With the sails hoisted and waves subsiding, the expedition gains some speed. The rough sea that had tossed the raft through the night now gently rocks the boat.

The crew settles down the best they can, savoring the peaceful surroundings. They need to rest and regain strength for the next day. They sit on the inner tubes and lean on the side rails. The exhaustion of almost six hours of non-stop rowing and the drowsiness caused by a motion sickness medication taken before leaving the house make them feel lethargic. The isolated, serene landscape and the swaying movement of the raft plunge them all into a deep sleep.

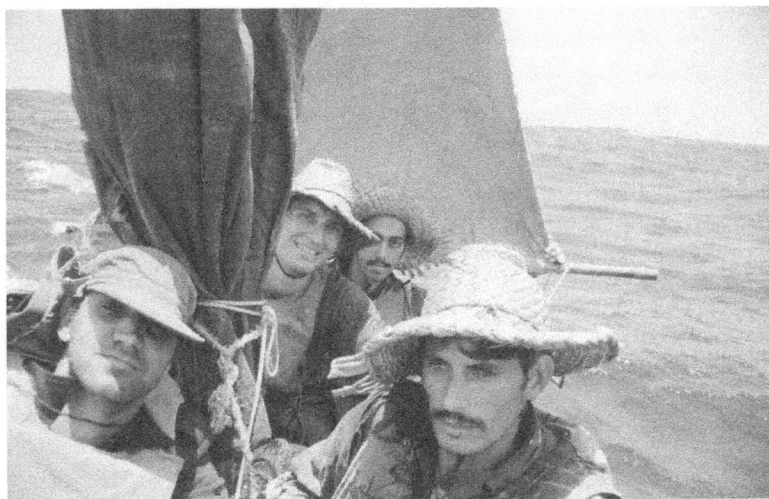

From left to right: Gonzalez, Gerardo, Roberto, and Raul. In the background, the jib is fully open. The mainsail remains furled. Photo taken from the stern, by Carlos.

Gerardo (left) and Roberto (right) celebrating after confirming the sails work.

5

THE NEXT DAY

"You guys are crazy!" Zady's voice echoes in Roberto's mind.

"No, sister. I've planned everything very well. We're gonna make it."

"It's just that I can't believe it," Zady says, her head shaking negatively. "I'm helping you, but I still think you're crazy."

"Son…" his mother, Carmen, interrupts. "I believe in you, but why are you wobbling like that?"

"Wobbling…? Me…?" Confusion seizes Roberto, forcing him to wake up. "Shit! We're too close to Havana," he mutters.

Morro Castle's lighthouse gleams on the horizon about eight miles south, its powerful beacon emitting two light beams sweeping the sky every fifteen seconds. Built in 1845, the castle guards like a sentinel over the port entrance, with its colossal lighthouse rising forty-four meters above sea level.

The city's lights also shine on the horizon, and when a wave lifts the raft, the crew catches glimpses of the street lighting casting an intermittent line along Malecon Avenue.

"We're screwed!" Carlos says, a hint of a joke in his voice. "It's almost dawn, and we haven't lost the coast yet."

Carlos's teammates laugh, but despite the lighthearted tone, they know the danger of being spotted by the island's Coast Guard.

"Guys, we must lose sight of the coast before sunrise," Carlos says as he positions his oar.

Roberto pulls a German-made compass from his cargo pants' pocket and hands it to Gonzalez at the helm.

"Here! It's about time you used it."

The compass comprises two pieces: a base and a lid with a circular mirror inside. The base comprises a transparent cylinder, about four centimeters in diameter by one centimeter high, called the rotating housing. Filled with oil, the rotating housing contains a magnetic needle, which always points north. The edge of the rotating housing has a 360-degree scale marked in phosphorescent green for night reading. This scale allows the user to calculate an azimuth, an angle formed clockwise between magnetic north and any other direction. For this expedition, however, the latter function is irrelevant because they are heading north; they just have to follow the magnetic needle.

Gonzalez takes the precious instrument in a small, black plastic box and hangs it around his neck.

"Let's boost our energy before we start," Gerardo says, grabbing the bottle containing the cloying mixture.

"I think that's a good idea," Gonzalez nods in agreement.

The first light of dawn tinges the eastern horizon, announcing that sunrise is just a couple of hours away.

After drinking the sweet mixture, the crew members take their places and begin rowing. To their surprise, they see dozens of tiny green phosphorescent lights swirling under and around the raft. The lights appear and disappear in the small whirlpools created by the oars and the inner tubes. They look like a swarm of fireflies dancing in the dark waters. The sight is both beautiful and eerie.

"Man, what are those lights down there?" Gonzalez asks, his voice trembling.

"Don't know, bro, but if they're scaring you that much, don't look at them," Gerardo says, shrugging.

"Gonzalez!" Roberto intervenes, his voice firm. "Don't worry about the lights. Focus on the compass and the rudder."

As they row, the crew tries to find an explanation for the strange lights. Roberto and Gerardo conclude some microorganisms in the water emit these phosphorescent lights when shaken. Though they are not sure, their explanation quells the crew's curiosity.

The expedition presses on as the first golden light of sunrise appears on the eastern horizon. Toward the south, Havana sinks slowly into the sea; now, only El Morro's lighthouse and the upper part of the tallest buildings are still visible above the water's surface.

The darkness covering the sky recedes as a new celestial landscape emerges. Its color tones range from bluish-gray in the west to intense gold in the east. The once infinite blackness of the sea changes to a blue-indigo hue, revealing its depth.

"It's getting brighter! We must lower the sails," Roberto says.

The oars stop in unison, and the crew springs into action. The two brothers pick up the jib, retract the mainsail, and roll it over the mast. Gerardo and Raul release the two backstay lines at the stern while Roberto leans toward the bow and releases the forestay. Meanwhile, kneeling at the center of the raft, Carlos pulls the mast out of its base, places it crosswise on the raft, and firmly ties it. They work with quick efficiency; a few drills at Carmen's house prepared them for this. Besides, the challenging experience of setting the sail up in the early morning darkness further improves the young crew's skills.

The four rowers return to their positions, and the journey continues. With both sails down, it will be harder for a patrol boat to spot them because the four rowers are sitting close to the water.

Like golden arrows, the first sun's rays cross the sky, making their way through the multitude of clouds as an incandescent orange ring emerges behind the eastern horizon.

"The sun is coming out," they cheer.

The crew row as the magnificent sunrise captures their attention, and they are in awe as they admire the beauty of the moment. Just as they are taking in the breathtaking scenery, Carlos interrupts with a sudden cry.

"Look!" Carlos says, his arm outstretched, gesturing toward the east.

A small gray dot next to the rising sun reveals a ship's presence.

"It must be the damn Coast Guard. They're coming for us," Raul says, the alarm clear in his voice.

The team agrees with Raul.

The group has learned some strategies employed by the Coast Guard through stories heard from other rafters. Frequently, they use night surveillance equipment to locate those who have evaded the iron-clad land control. Then, the next morning, taking advantage of the rafts' slow sailing speed, the Coast Guard sends speedboats to intercept them.

"Well, let them catch us rowing," Gerardo shouts defiantly, refusing to back down.

"You bet!" Roberto agrees as he squeezes his oar and instructs the helmsman. "Gonzalez, move to a lower spot."

With the mast down, the helmsman's seat is the raft's highest position, reaching four feet above sea level, and the team doesn't want to give up. The Coast Guard hasn't captured them yet.

The crew rows harder, their strength fueled by frustration and rage against a regime that oppresses and keeps its people in misery. Piercing gazes, furrowed eyebrows, and raised chins on the crew's faces show the group's defiance. The Coast Guard has yet to find them, and they're determined not to give up.

The expedition continues its marathon route, with the crew's eyes fixed on the growing gray dot on the horizon.

"That doesn't look like the Coast Guard's boat," Carlos says, a hint of optimism in his words.

"I don't think so," Gerardo adds. "They would have been here by now."

"Besides, the ship is still quite far away, and yet, look how big it is. It has to be a merchant ship," Roberto suggests.

"I hope you're right," Raul says.

As time does not stop and the unknown ship approaches, their fear of it being a maritime patrol diminishes. Meanwhile, Esperanza continues her journey north while the ship, sailing west, will intercept the raft in roughly half an hour.

The gray dot has already taken on colors and shapes. To their surprise, it is a tourist cruise ship sailing parallel to the north coast of Havana, about eighteen miles from shore. Its passengers marvel at Havana from the top deck, the legendary metropolis, the forbidden city that once was the most prosperous in the Caribbean.

"Dang, that's a huge ship! It's beautiful! Never seen anything like it!"

The ship's magnificent presence leaves the young men in awe, and the crew can't stop talking about its remarkable architecture.

The massive ship gets closer and closer, sailing just a few hundred yards away from the raft.

"It's stopping!" Carlos says with excitement.

The foamy white waves under the ship's bow gradually diminish until they disappear. The raft's crew stops rowing, and the expedition halts, cautiously keeping a safe distance from the unknown ship.

"Raul! Get the camera and take some pictures," Roberto asks his friend.

Almost a year before, Raul shared his vision with Roberto to document their journey. Since then, Raul, being an amateur photographer, has captured each milestone in their quest using his old, 35mm-film, Soviet-made camera he carries in his backpack.

"Forget about the camera, man," Raul says with anguish. "My backpack went underwater at the beach, and I don't think the camera survived."

"Hey, I think they've seen us," Gonzalez says enthusiastically.

"What country is it from?" Gerardo asks.

Roberto replies, scanning the deck for a flag. "I don't know. All I see are party flags." He refers to the multi-colored flags used to decorate the ship during its festivities.

"Well, it's definitely not Cuban," Gonzalez quips.

"Guys, it doesn't matter where it's from. It stopped to pick us up," Raul says, showing his disposition to board the cruise.

"But what if it takes us to Mexico? They might send us back to Cuba," Roberto is distrustful.

"That's true," Carlos and Gerardo concur.

"I'll do what you guys decide, but my vote is to get on board," Raul's proposal is tempting.

"I don't know, man," Roberto says. "This ship is going west, toward Mexico. It could change its course later, but we don't know. What I know for sure is we trained hard for two years, and I don't want to risk going back to Cuba."

The men huddle together, murmuring about their options while the towering cruise ship looms in front of them. With much deliberation, the crew finally reaches a consensus.

"I think we should keep going," Carlos says, placing his oar in the water.

"Me too," Gerardo follows suit.

Raul hesitates, then nods in agreement. "I trust you guys, and I know we'll make it, so let's go!"

"Let's do it!" the team declares.

The men take their positions, ready to continue their journey.

"We'll go around, behind the ship," Roberto directs.

Gonzalez turns the rudder, the oars splash, and the raft moves, pivoting toward the cruise ship's stern. Meanwhile, the crew of the majestic ship stands bewildered, watching as the small craft intentionally sails away. It's the first time a group of rafters has chosen to continue their journey in their precarious boat rather than boarding a luxurious cruise ship.

Half an hour later, the ship engines start. Its propellers' action produces white-water turbulence under the ship's stern. The grand vessel resumes its tour, leaving the intrepid rafters behind. The men watch the exotic ship with wonder, their first glimpse of the outside world forbidden to them by the Cuban government. Rowing in silence, they each ponder their action. Have they made the right decision? Despite their uncertainties, they row with determination, setting their sights on the unknown horizon.

The sun blazes high overhead with a noon glow that warms the crew. They've been rowing without pause, and the majestic cruiser is a distant memory, vanished beyond the horizon.

"I'm starving! It's time to eat something," Gerardo says.

"Right! In the meantime, Gonzalez, pass me the bottle with diesel. I'll tie it to the bow. Don't want any visitors." Roberto refers to sharks, which are abundant in these waters.

"Where is the bottle?" Gonzalez asks.

"Inside a backpack, but I don't know which one," Roberto replies.

Gonzalez checks through the backpacks and pulls out the bottle of diesel, but as he does, he realizes the mistake Roberto has made.

"Oh, no! You put the diesel in the food backpack," Gonzalez says as he passes the bottle.

"Did I? No way!" Roberto realizes the cost of his mistake.

"Everything is contaminated with diesel," Gonzalez confirms his friend's fear.

During the hasty escape, Roberto had put the bottle of diesel in the nearest backpack, not realizing it contained the food.

The young man crawls to the bow and ties the bottle to the raft's structure just below the waterline. Through the bottle's cloth cap, drops of fuel leak, forming a shapeless and colorful stain on the sea surface around the bow. While there, Roberto looks down. He contemplates the spectacular deep blue water below. Sun rays pierce the liquid mass and fade into the infinite. Nearly 6,000 feet down, in perpetual darkness, is the seafloor. It is beautiful but terrifying. Then, he remembers Jaws, the infamous megalodon from the movie he watched when he was nine when his grandfather sneaked him into the theater. A shiver runs down his spine as he imagines a large predator stalking him from below.

"Nope! That's not gonna happen." Roberto rejects his doom-filled thought and returns to his front rower seat next to his brother.

Meanwhile, Gonzalez, Raul, and Gerardo salvage what they can from the contaminated backpack. They separate the boiled eggs, peanut nougat bars, and guava paste pieces, washing them with seawater and placing them in another backpack. They also dispose of everything they deem spoiled.

"Shit! This is pure diesel," Raul laughs after trying a piece of a peanut nougat bar.

"We're gonna be like stoves burning diesel," Carlos says, referring to the unpleasant smell produced by kerosene stoves commonly used in Cuba.

"We should throw the one who did this overboard," Gerardo teases Roberto.

"I'm sorry, guys. In such a hurry, I didn't realize it was the food backpack." Roberto apologizes, embarrassed.

"It doesn't matter to me; with or without diesel, I'll eat it. Besides, we still have the water and sugar." Gonzalez shows his insatiable appetite.

The men quickly mock the situation, laughing and even celebrating that the water and sugar container was not contaminated. They maintain their optimism and confidence in the expedition's success.

During their physiology lectures at the Sports University, Roberto and Gerardo learned how prolonged physical activities affect the human body. When glucose levels in the bloodstream decrease because of extended work and insufficient nutrition, the nervous system is affected, causing fatigue and dizziness. Consequently, they relied on a diet of water and sugar, supplemented with vitamins, honey, lemon juice, rehydration salts, and bread, in addition to the sweets and boiled eggs the diesel had damaged.

"Guys, look ahead," Gonzalez says, pointing toward the horizon.

The horizon's straight line has morphed into a jagged surface, a shifting mountain range of water peaks.

"That's got to be..." Roberto trails off, taking a brief pause "...the Gulf Stream."

"Bro, we had no idea it was that strong," Gerardo says.

As the raft approaches the Gulf Stream, the crew braces themselves for the challenge ahead. They have read articles about the Florida Straits and its dangerous Gulf Stream. Although they know it is one of the strongest ocean currents in the world, they expected the change in water speed to be gradual, hardly perceptible. The reality, however, is quite different. The powerful stream announces its presence with a drastic change on the horizon as a surface sea current created by the stormy winds moving west collides with the Gulf Stream, a much stronger current running in the opposite direction. The collision of both currents creates a turbulent sea with round, bubble-like waves reaching an average height of six feet.

"We gotta go into that with all we've got," Gerardo says.

"We trained hard for this, didn't we?" Carlos seems thrilled by the challenge.

"Who wants to go back, anyway?" Raul jokes.

"Turning back? Only dead," Gonzalez says.

"Gonzalez, go switch places with Raul so he can take a break," the navigator instructs the helmsman.

"Sure."

"Hey, hang on, I'm not done yet," Raul appeals.

"I know you're good," Roberto nods, "but you should take a break."

"I agree, Raul. Go take a break," Gerardo says.

"Okay," Raul accepts, giving the job to his cousin and crawling toward the helmsman's position.

Of all the crew members, Raul is the most impacted by the hunger and malnutrition that torments countless Cubans. At a height of five feet ten inches, he weighs only 113 pounds. His acromioclavicular joints protrude from his anorexic body, and for this reason, his friends agree he should take the first break.

Gonzalez settles into his new position and takes hold of the oar.

"I'm ready," he announces.

The four oars flap and the expedition resumes its march, but something is amiss. Gonzalez struggles to synchronize his movements, causing Esperanza to stop again.

"Listen!" says Gerardo, who is sitting next to Gonzalez. "Look at me. Let's row together. Forward when I go, and pull when I pull."

"Calm down, man. I'm just warming up," Gonzalez jokes.

"Raul, count to four so Gonzalez can follow the pace," Roberto says.

"Good idea! Are you ready?" Raul asks.

"Go ahead," Gonzalez says.

Once again, the small boat moves. The count helps Gonzalez row to his friends' rhythm. However, he lacks technique, and the abrupt impact of his oar on the sea surface splashes water onto the bow rowers.

"Gonzalez!" Roberto calls out to the inexperienced oarsman. "You can't throw the oar back. You're splashing too much water."

"How do I do it then?" Gonzalez asks.

"Hey, easy with your oar. You're splashing me," Roberto exclaims.

"I can't believe someone from Santa Fe, two blocks from the coast, doesn't know how to row," Gerardo mocks his friend.

"Sorry, guys. I've never rowed in my life," Gonzalez apologizes.

"Well, learn fast because we have a long route ahead," Carlos says.

A few minutes later...

"No way, I can't take this anymore," Roberto's oar stops. "If this guy keeps throwing water on me, I'm gonna drown."

The other oars also stop, and Esperanza comes to a halt.

"Sorry, man, didn't have time to train with you," Gonzalez says, embarrassed.

"Hey, hey, I've rested enough," Raul interrupts. "I'll take it from here."

"I think it'll be better," Carlos agrees.

"Okay. Gonzalez, go back to the rudder," Roberto instructs.

Although his break lasted just a few minutes, Raul is eager to return to the rowing post. The two young men exchange their positions again; Gonzalez goes back to the helm, and Raul returns to the oar.

"Alright!" Gerardo chants.

The four oars beat in sync, and the expedition advances toward its destination.

As they reach the point where the coastal current meets the Gulf Stream, the sea surface becomes turbulent, with spontaneous eddies forming everywhere. The ocean resembles water boiling in a cauldron only here, the bubbles are gigantic. Esperanza shakes. Sometimes, it rises up to six feet on top of a water burst; other times, it slides into a funnel, which, like the liquid eruptions, appears and disappears instantly.

The turbulent sea proves to be a formidable opponent, but the crew is undeterred and continues rowing, although it is almost impossible for them to keep up. The abrupt changes in the sea's surface are sudden. Now, the oars are used to give Esperanza stability as well as propelling her. But this is not enough. The crew must stay on the lookout, prepared to rush quickly toward the raft's rising side that rises. They avoid capsizing by shifting their weight across the vessel. If the boat capsizes, they will be unable to control the vessel and navigate; they will be adrift. Despite the danger, the five men are optimistic and maintain their sense of humor.

"This feels like a freakin' roller coaster," Roberto says, a tone of joy in his voice.

"So, is this the famous Gulf Stream? The beast isn't as terrible as it looks," Carlos shows off his adventurous spirit.

It's already noon, and the weather has worsened again. The sun hides behind a blanket of cobbled clouds, unwilling to witness the dangerous adventure. However, from time to time, it sends its warm rays through isolated holes as a sign of sympathy toward the intrepid people on the sea.

The expedition overcomes the turbulent area where the two sea currents collide. They have left the chaotic water spurts and funnels behind as they venture into the Gulf Stream, heading deep into the fearsome Strait of Death, a notorious nickname assigned because thousands of Cubans have lost their lives crossing it.

The Gulf Stream, the fastest deep ocean current in the world, reaches a speed of 5.6 mph at its narrow passage between Cuba and the Florida peninsula. Viewed from the air, it appears like a river inside the ocean. The vast sea torrent flows toward the east before reaching the Atlantic Ocean and turning north.

The sea surface is now more stable, although it moves opposite to the wind direction. This increases the wind's speed relative to the ocean's surface, causing enormous waves, which sometimes exceed twelve feet in height.

The restless sea turns into an army of waves whose ends go beyond the horizon. However, not everything is a setback. Sailing is less dangerous because the sea becomes more stable and predictable. Although the gigantic waves are larger than the previous water spurts and funnels, they do not form spontaneously. Created by the strong wind, they always strike from the starboard (right) side. Also, the waves advance in the opposite direction to the sea current, making the liquid walls move extremely slowly. Hence, the force of their impact against the raft is reduced, and the young crew have more time to act. It feels like riding a slow, never-ending roller coaster sideways.

"Have you examined these waves?" Gerardo asks Roberto.

"Yeah. I've been checking them out."

"It seems they're coming in slow motion," Gerardo says.

"M-hmm!" Roberto nods.

"Thank goodness they're slow 'cause they're ugly," Raul remarks.

"How about we set the sails?" Carlos asks.

It's almost one in the afternoon, and the crew rows on in silence and contemplation, their eyes fixed on the horizon. On land, they had agreed to hoist the sails at sunset. By then, they would be far enough from shore so the Cuban Coast Guard could not see the raft's sails on the horizon. Nevertheless, Carlos's premature proposal is tempting, and the men are growing impatient.

"We gotta catch up on the time we lost last night," Carlos presses.

Gerardo makes use of his skills as an instigator. "Bro... I'm dying to see the sails in action."

"I don't wanna risk being seen," Roberto says. He designed the raft, and no one could handle the sails better than him. So, everyone waits for his approval.

"They wouldn't try to catch anyone in this weather. I mean, come on, bro," Gerardo shrugs off Roberto's concerns.

"They probably won't, but…" Roberto remains silent for a moment. "Let's do it!" he concludes, accepting the challenge.

Already anticipating these words, the crew springs into action, quickly retrieving the oars and untying the mast and sail. Standing on their knees to maintain balance, the two brothers raise the mast vertically while Gerardo and Raul hold them steady so the constant jolts the raft receives do not throw them overboard. Meanwhile, at the helm, Gonzalez is to call out when a wave large enough to capsize the boat approaches. The respite between the onslaught of one wave and the next lasts only seconds. However, the crew knows they need to take advantage of these precious time intervals, so they hurry.

The brothers introduce the lower part of the mast into the base's hole and let it slide until it fits into the ball bearing, its resting position for the rest of the journey. They tie the three tensors destined to secure the mast. As before, the crew arranges two lines on the raft's stern and a third line on the bow's right corner. Next, the brothers unfurl the jib, the smaller sail, and provisionally settle it until they set the mainsail. Raul and Gerardo hold the boom in place while Carlos ties the boom to the mast. Then, Carlos pulls the halyard attached to the outer corner of the sail.

The line slides through the small pulley at the boom's outer end, pulling the sail out. Simultaneously, Roberto unravels the hoops holding the sail by its lower edge, so the hoop system unfurls like a shower curtain along the boom.

These hoops, about six inches in diameter, are used to unfurl or retract the mainsail along the boom. They are made of a medium-thickness rope and arranged at twelve-inch intervals along the mainsail's foot.

"Ready!" Carlos announces as the sail reaches its limit.

He secures the halyard to the boom's end, right where it joins the mast.

Pushed by the wind, the mast pivots until the sail reaches a 90-degree angle to the raft. There, the sail's canvas waves loose.

Roberto crawls back to the bow to finish setting up the jib. From there, he instructs his brother as he releases Carlos's safety cord so he can reach the raft's stern.

"Be careful. I'm untying your safety rope. Take one of the boom's tensors and go to the stern."

"Okay. Let me secure my line first."

Carlos ties his security rope to the mast base. From there, he can reach any section of the raft. Then, he crawls to the stern, bringing one boom's tensor line.

"Pull the sail till it's no longer waving," Roberto says.

Carlos sits in the stern and pulls the rope tied to the boom's outer end, making the mainsail turn until the wind swells its triangular canvas. The small boat resumes its movement, but now, it sails faster than when they were rowing.

"Is it okay like this?" Carlos asks.

"Yeah! Right there!" his brother says. "Now, I need someone here because there's too much weight back there," instructs the young navigator while he adjusts the jib's angle parallel to the mainsail.

"I'll move next to you," Gerardo volunteers as he releases his safety rope.

"Here comes a big one!" Gonzalez alerts his friends as another huge wave approaches.

Gerardo rushes to take up his new position before being hit by the liquid force. He has no time to tie his safety line, so he clings with tenacity to the raft's structure.

Just as Gerardo sits down in his new position, another massive wave lifts the raft. As they ascend the liquid hill, the raft's right side rises about thirty degrees, so the crew quickly shifts their weight to starboard to keep the raft balanced. The small boat levels out momentarily at the crest before initiating the descent behind the wave. During the descent, the inclination angle reverts, and the crew shifts their weight to the opposite side.

The youngsters maneuver with incredible speed, skill, and coordination; it's a race for survival. They must overcome nature's obstacles and conquer a formidable opponent: the Gulf Stream. Despite their inexperience, they are determined to reach their goal.

Gerardo secures his safety rope to the side rail next to the bow, ensuring he won't be swept overboard.

"Is your line secure?" Roberto asks his brother.

"Yep!" Carlos replies. "I'm tying the boom now."

"Gonzalez, pass the compass to Carlos and go sit next to Raul," the navigator instructs.

Gonzalez moves to his new spot, balancing out the weight distribution of the raft.

"You know… I think it's time to eat something," Gonzalez suggests mischievously.

"You're right!" the idea catches on, and everyone cheers.

"I'm gonna get the vitamins," Raul says as he opens the backpack that almost drowned him the night before.

"I hope they didn't get ruined from getting wet," Gerardo refers to the episode at the beach when Raul almost drowned.

Raul pulls out a plastic bag containing the camera to reach the vitamins.

"What if…?" Raul thinks. His curiosity ignites, leading him to take out the black leather case and open it to check the camera. To his amazement, he finds the light-recording instrument is in perfect condition.

"Oh, man! You're not gonna believe this."

"What happened?" his friends ask.

"The camera… it didn't get wet."

"I thought you said it was messed up?" Roberto asks.

"That's what I thought," Raul explains with enthusiasm. "The backpack was underwater, the plastic bag wrapping the camera had holes, and the case isn't waterproof. It's a miracle the camera is dry."

"Well then, take pictures," Roberto says. "Give it to Carlos so he can shoot one from the bow."

Raul hands the camera over and makes his way to the boat's stern to snap some pictures.

"Come closer… a little more. Nice!"

The young crew takes their food rations, which comprise vitamins 'C' and 'complex B,' sweets, and the cloying mixture of water, sugar, honey, and lemon.

"These sweets won't last because of the salt water. Let's eat them now," Gerardo advises.

"Of course!" Gonzalez agrees. "It'd be a shame to waste them."

While Gerardo and Gonzalez eat the last sweets, Raul turns to Carlos.

"Can you pass me the camera? I gotta get a pic of that wave."

Carlos hands Raul the camera, and Raul carries out his duties as the expedition's photographer.

"Let's make funny faces," Roberto says while he and Gerardo pose next to the mast with cheerful expressions.

"Perfect!" Raul says, activating the camera shutter.

With the sails working as expected and Esperanza moving fast, the men are in high spirits. The exhausting paddling quest has now turned into an exciting adventure. Despite having no experience in navigation, the young crew steers the boat using the sails, transforming the strong wind into their ally as it pushes the expedition toward its goal.

After eating their rations and joking for a while, the young rafters take a break. They accommodate themselves as best they can, maintaining their weight distribution on the raft. Carlos remains at the helm, controlling the course of the boat with the compass in hand.

"Course?" Roberto asks his brother from time to time to ensure the expedition stays on track.

"North," he answers over and over.

The expedition has entered a new stage of its journey, with reduced physical activity since they no longer have to row. Instead, they focus on maintaining the raft's balance and watching their surroundings. If a shark approaches, they must detect its presence in time to repel a potential attack. Fortunately, this last possibility is relatively unlikely because the sea is remarkably rough. Apparently, sharks prefer to stay away from rough surfaces to avoid being tossed around by the waves. Since they are not rowing, the crew members now have time to reflect on their current reality.

"How's everyone doing back home?" Roberto asks, referring to the surveillance team left behind, his thoughts momentarily straying from their perilous journey.

"Worried sick about us, no doubt," Gerardo says, the memory of his father's heart-breaking goodbye fresh in his mind.

"I can only imagine," Roberto nods. "Yesterday, Radio Martí warned of two-meter waves in the Gulf. Yet here we are, taking pictures like we're on a vacation."

"Bro…" Gerardo chuckles. "I think the meteorologists got it wrong because the waves seem even bigger. But hey, at least we're finally going on the tourist tour we never had."

Just then, Roberto's expression changes as he doubles over the wooden rail, retching. The same motion that keeps sharks at bay leaves the crew vulnerable to seasickness.

"Are you alright?" Gerardo asks, holding his friend's arm.

"I'm fine. It's passed," the young man recovers quickly, rinsing his face with salt water and slapping his right cheek. "Can't let that happen again."

"Sure you're okay?" Gerardo insists.

"I'm good."

The expedition pushes on, venturing northward into the unknown, always looking for a new horizon beyond what their eyes can see. To lift their spirits and distract themselves from their hazardous reality, they sing songs by Willy Chirino and John Secada. Despite being banned by the Communist regime, these songwriters were acclaimed by the Cuban youth. They also share stories and jokes. Raul, however, remains silent; his face is pale, and his gaze is fixed on the horizon.

"What's up, man? Missing your girlfriend already?" Roberto teases Raul, trying to distract him.

"No, I've felt dizzy for a while," Raul says.

During their training sessions, his friends realized he was the most prone to motion sickness.

"Look at a fixed point," Gerardo advises Raul.

"That's what I'm doing."

Despite his dire situation, Raul remains stoic, neither complaining nor smiling. His friends attempt to lighten the mood by joking to hide their concerns and cheer Raul up. They know if the crisis worsens and triggers vomiting, it could lead to Raul's dehydration because of his low body weight. His scant 113 pounds, contrasting with his 5-foot 10-inch height and the almost total lack of body fat, which makes up the body's main energy reserve, represents a real danger to Raul's survival.

But Raul's condition worsens, and he starts vomiting.

As the group's doctor, Gerardo rushes into action.

"Sit in the center of the raft and lean against the mast. Gonzalez, pass me the bottle of water with rehydration salts and the motion sickness pills."

Gonzalez takes a two-liter plastic bottle from the medicine backpack with a mixture of water, dextrose, rehydration salts, and lemon juice and hands it to Gerardo.

"Rinse your face with seawater and drink this," Gerardo administers Raul a pill and the bottle with the mixture.

Raul follows Gerardo's instructions, but minutes later, the vomiting returns. His friend hands him the bottle once again, urging him to drink more of the rehydration solution.

"You think he threw up the pill?" Roberto asks Gerardo.

"I'm almost sure he has, but I'm afraid to give him another pill and knock him down. For now, I'm going to give him liquid, and if he keeps vomiting, then I'll give him another pill."

After a while, Raul's health improves, and he overcomes the crisis. But their troubles are not over yet. Carlos, who is at the helm, spots a fist-sized hole in the mainsail.

"Guys!" the young man says to his companions. "There's a hole in the sail. We must fix it before it gets bigger."

As the onboard mechanic, Carlos is tasked with ensuring the raft's structure stays in good shape. In fact, he is the one in charge of repairing anything that breaks. Through his profession as a truck driver and his experience as a fisherman, he is highly skilled with ropes and knots.

"How did the sail get ripped?" Gerardo asks, surprised.

"No idea," Roberto says.

"Let's see what I can use to repair it," Carlos says, searching through his backpack.

"Use the needle and suture thread in the first-aid kit," his brother suggests.

"I think I have something better. Here it is!" Carlos says as he extracts a small coil of copper wire.

"You take care of the hole, and I'll control the sail," Roberto says.

"I'll help you with the hole," Gerardo volunteers.

After being relieved by his brother, Carlos moves to the center of the raft, where Gerardo is already waiting for him. Holding onto the mast, Carlos uses a nail to perforate tiny holes in the canvas around the gap. Then, Gerardo passes the copper wire through the tiny holes from the opposite side of the sail. Carlos pulls the wire, tightens it, and returns it to Gerardo through another perforation. Stitch after stitch, the gap decreases until the hole is closed.

With the repair complete, Gerardo returns to the front rower seat next to Raul, and Carlos sits next to Gonzalez.

The afternoon is no longer young. The sun has been descending, peeking its golden ring occasionally through the thick clouds.

"It's about six in the afternoon. How far have we sailed?" Gerardo asks the group's navigator.

"About thirty miles, perhaps."

"That's it?"

"Remember, we spent all night trying to get off the coast."

Roberto's original estimate was that they would have sailed about forty miles by then. However, bad weather during the escape caused the expedition to go off course, adding several hours to their original plans.

The wind, which had remained somewhat serene during the morning, blows stronger in the afternoon. The crew has become used to the up-and-down pattern of the waves. On one of these ascents, when the raft reaches the top of a wave, Gerardo points to the east and warns the group, "I think I saw a guy in the water.".

"What?" his friends ask, looking to the east where Gerardo points.

"Let's go over there," Roberto suggests.

During their training, the crew discussed the possibility of helping other rafters they might encounter at sea. They have enough water and sugar reserves and a first-aid kit. Furthermore, the three members studying at the Sports University have some knowledge of water rescue and CPR techniques.

"No, wait!" Gerardo exclaims. "What I saw was floating in the water. If it was a guy, he'll be dead and probably decomposed, and that attracts sharks."

"Oh," Roberto retracts. "I thought you saw someone on a raft."

The crew scans the water, trying to locate any signs of the supposed body, but the restless sea prevents it. The waves look like barricades, allowing only small strips of the surface to be seen between one wave and the next.

"There!" Raul exclaims in one of those fleeting moments when a wave lifts Esperanza. "I think I saw a man in a blue shirt, but I lost sight of him right away."

"That's what I saw," Gerardo says.

The other members say they have seen nothing.

With every passing second, the chance of seeing the supposed body decreases. Besides facilitating holding their course, the wind prevents the raft from being pulled by the sea current to the east, but anything else floating on the surface will be dragged away by the ocean flow. This is why when Raul saw the alleged body, it was further away than when Gerardo saw it.

After a few minutes of fruitless observation, the crew gives up the search.

"There is nothing we can do."

For the next hours, the five young men remain silent, consumed by their thoughts. They contemplate the vastness of the ocean and the smallness of their raft. They wonder about the man they saw, if he had a family waiting for him, if he was another victim of the circumstances making a desperate choice to escape the island. The crew thinks about the countless others who may have suffered a similar fate, lost at sea and forgotten. Their silence speaks volumes as they are left to grapple with the weight of their mortality and the fragility of life.

The sunset is a magnificent display of beauty. Golden light rays pierce the clouds and stretch across the celestial space, dissolving behind the looming cumulus clouds in the eastern sky. The landscape becomes a mixture of warm and cold colors in perfect harmony. It is a heavenly masterpiece, evoking a sense of melancholy in the young crew. They take this moment of peace to reflect on everything they have left behind - home, family, loved ones, and cherished memories. However, despite the nostalgia, the five intrepid rafters remain resolute. They know this is the price they must pay for the simple desire to live in freedom, without hatred or humiliation, and for the urgent need to help their families mitigate hunger. It is precisely this need that makes them strong and determined to move forward with their eyes fixed on the future and the hope of triumph.

Raul scans the horizon. In the background, at the stern, Carlos controls the rudder. Gonzalez peeks out from behind the mast. Photo taken by Roberto from the bow.

Raft's stern view. From left to right: Gonzalez, Raul, and Roberto. Note the inner tubes wrapped with strips of sacks to protect them from the sun, chunks of wood, etc. Photo taken by Carlos.

The Gulf Stream and its rough waters. Photo taken by Raul.

6

THE TIDE

Swallowed whole by the horizon, the sun disappears, but its golden rays seep through the western clouds before fading into the sky's endless abyss. To the east, a darker steel-blue veil dominates the heavenly dome, casting a gray-blue hue across the sea's surface. The water reflects the darkening sky above, absorbing all light and color. Venus announces the night is imminent. The wind howls like a pack of wolves, whipping the sea into a frenzy, each wave crashing like thunder against the raft.

"This thing is flying!" Roberto says, amazed by the raft's speed. "If we continue like this, we'll get there soon."

As the young crew prepares to face a second night, they secure the moorings and check their backpacks. They know how dark and unpredictable the sea can be.

————⟨⟨✟⟩⟩————

Time passes, and the night enters with its dark entrails as the colorful sunset fades into a dense darkness. Now and then, the moon's silver edge and a few stars peek through the clouds.

The expedition advances through the black void, navigating almost blindly with the aid of the compass. They can no longer see beyond their noses. A faint, phosphorescent dot at the tip of the magnetic needle guides them to the north, and when the clouds permit, they use Polaris, the North Star, to confirm their course.

Carlos glances at his wristwatch, and the numbers on the dial glow in the dark; it's almost 10 o'clock. The expedition is about to complete its first 24 hours at sea. The sky turns ashen red, and the wind's intensity increases dangerously. Esperanza sails at a remarkable speed, but the roaring swell grows more violent, pounding harder and harder against the inner tubes and the wooden structure.

"If this wind continues, we'll have to lower the sails," Roberto shouts, concern evident in his voice. "The mast won't hold up; it'll break."

The group's navigator has been checking the lines holding the main mast and the sail, and he notices their tension is reaching breaking point.

"They look like guitar strings," Roberto says, his voice tinged with worry.

"What a pity we have to lose this momentum," Carlos laments.

"It's too risky. If the mast breaks, then we're screwed," Roberto says. "We can leave the jib on for now."

Finally, everyone agrees to retract the mainsail and continue with the smaller one. Roberto unties the rope guiding the large sail while Carlos and Gerardo work to retract and furl the sail on the mast. With each inch of canvas they pull in, the raft slows, and its bow turns westward, pushed by the howling wind.

"What about the boom? Should I retract it, too?" Carlos asks his brother.

"No, just tie it up so it won't hit anyone."

Carlos grapples with the boom, his muscles straining as he fights to keep it steady against the relentless onslaught of the swell. The small boat bucks and heaves beneath him, but he holds on, determined to keep the long spar from swaying in the powerful shocks.

"I'm going to turn the raft with the oar," Carlos announces, taking one oar and sitting in the front-left oarsman's position.

Carlos rows, but the force of the stormy wind battering the smaller sail prevents him from bringing the bow to the north.

Roberto shouts at the crew member closest to the bow, "Raul, release the jib so we can turn the raft."

Raul unties the tensor line, freeing the smaller sail. "Done."

The jib waves like a flag beaten by an invisible force. The raft's wind resistance decreases, and, with a great effort from Carlos, the vessel changes its course.

"Set the jib now!" Roberto directs the two crew members at the bow.

Raul and Gerardo set the smaller sail again and fix it with its corresponding guiding ropes. Contrary to what the crew expects, Esperanza turns west again.

"Something is wrong," Roberto reflects. "We've got too much weight at the front! Raul, go to the stern and row backward."

The crew does not give up and repeats the maneuver. Gerardo takes control of the jib this time, and Raul moves to the rear-right oarsman position and rows backward. By rowing in the opposite direction, he aids Carlos in turning the boat.

The inexperienced sailors turn the bow to the north, but when they unfurl the smaller sail, the raft veers to the west again.

"Why?" Roberto wonders. "What are we doing wrong?"

The situation is serious, and there is no time to think. As the storm rages on, the powerful shocks threaten to capsize the vessel at any moment. The wind and salty water lash against their faces, dulling their senses as they struggle to keep the boat steady.

"Gerardo, pick up the jib and tie it up," Roberto commands. "We are gonna start rowing!"

Roberto gets ready to switch places with Gonzalez, who currently occupies the rear left rower position alongside Raul. Carlos adjusts his position toward the center of the raft to maneuver the two front oars while Gerardo furls and secures the smaller sail.

Carlos shouts. "There's an oar missing!"

"What?!" Roberto asks, his concern evident.

"We lost the right-front oar," Carlos confirms, a note of worry in his voice.

Carlos's announcement shocks the crew, especially Roberto, who returns to the helm and must quickly devise a new strategy.

Roberto remembers the lost oar is the same one that got entangled with its safety rope during the escape, and Carlos had to break the rope to free it.

"I can't believe we've lost an oar," Roberto thinks with regret, but as the expedition's navigator, he promptly acts. "Carlos, row with the left oar at the bow. Raul, you row with the right one in the back! And you, Gonzalez, set the third oar vertically in the water and hold it tight to give us stability. It's up to you not to let us capsize."

The crew follows Roberto's lead, working together as a team. During training, they created contingency plans for emergencies. They understand the importance of staying united if they hope to survive the treacherous journey ahead.

"To the right!" Gerardo shouts from the bow, alerting his friends fractions of seconds before receiving the impact of another wave.

The group cannot see the incoming waves in the darkness until they are almost upon them. To prevent being caught off guard, the young rafters rely on their hearing and the raft's movements to detect the approaching waves, which relentlessly batter the fragile structure.

The immense liquid wall crashes into the small vessel, causing the boat's bow to be pushed in a westerly direction once more. Since the bow is the lightest section of the boat, the force of the water easily sways it.

The young crew encourages each other as they try to reset the raft on course. "Let's turn her back again!"

When they almost succeed, another massive wave sends them back to their previous position. The determined crew remains resolute and continues to fight for survival against the relentless power of the sea.

As time progresses, the raging sea makes it difficult for the expedition to maintain its course. The powerful swells make rowing a challenge, and progress becomes nearly impossible.

"Guys, we are killing ourselves! I think we should stop rowing to conserve energy and wait for the storm to pass," Roberto says.

Gerardo agrees. "I think that'd be the best."

Carlos and Raul pick up their oars and tie them to the raft's structure to secure them.

"Gonzalez, don't let go of that oar," Roberto says. "If you do, we will capsize."

"I won't!"

"If you get tired, let someone know so they can relieve you."

Gonzalez is sitting at the rear-left rower seat, his grip firm on the vertically submerged oar. He squeezes the back end of the oar against his chest while he clings to the boat's side rail with equal determination.

After securing his oar, Raul makes his way to the front-left rower seat next to Gerardo, his rowing partner. Carlos then crawls to the rear oars and sits beside Gonzalez. The rowers' seats are the safest spots on the boat, as their proximity to the water's surface allows for better balance. There, the crew members are less likely to be thrown overboard by a wave. Roberto, no longer needing to man the helm, joins his brother and Gonzalez. He sits between the two men, tightly gripping their knees with a locked hand maneuver. Together, they form a human chain, each link protecting the other.

The weather continues to worsen. The swell mercilessly batters the small raft and attempts to claim its crew. But the five men remain seated and hunched forward with their heads tucked between their knees. They protect themselves from the relentless onslaught of the waves as they crash down on the crew like predatory birds. They cling to the raft like spiders to a web, desperate not to be swept out into the dark sea. The wind whipping their drenched bodies and their malnutrition and excessive exertion during the last twenty-four hours are taking their toll. Their energy wanes, and their bodies tremble as they feel the intense cold that comes with hypothermia. Their speech becomes slurred.

Roberto grabs three of the five light raincoats they have in one backpack. After giving one to Carlos and another to Gonzalez, he proceeds to put on his own. A tap on his shoulder comes from behind.

"What?" Roberto asks as he finishes adjusting his clothes. The tempestuous sea rocks the raft beneath him, and Roberto's mind is focused on his current task. Any distraction can lead to tragedy.

Gerardo remains silent for a few more seconds. Turning to see why his friend is not responding, Roberto insists. "What is it?"

"G-g-give me m-mine," Gerardo says, shivering.

Roberto catches sight of his friend's dark, trembling silhouette, struggling to speak. Swiftly, he takes another raincoat and hands it to Gerardo, who, with great difficulty, puts it on. Gerardo has succumbed to hypothermia; the cold has affected him more than the others as he is not wearing thick, durable military clothes like the rest of the crew. At his father's request, he wears a dark blue long-sleeved shirt made of thin fabric.

Sometime later, Gerardo calls out to Roberto again, his voice raspy and weak but more coherent than before. Roberto turns to check on his friend. He can't see Gerardo's face, but Roberto can tell his friend is recovering from his voice.

"Can you pass me the honey?"

Without hesitation, Roberto leans over and grabs the bottle of honey from the provisions backpack. He hands the bottle to Gerardo, who immediately takes two large gulps of the cloying mixture. Gerardo feels the dense liquid sliding down his throat and into his stomach. The thick syrup coats his esophagus as it descends, leaving a lingering sweetness in its wake. Gerardo closes the bottle and hands it back to Roberto.

"When I asked you for my raincoat, I couldn't even speak. I was freezing," Gerardo says, his teeth still chattering.

Roberto nods, understanding all too well. "I know. You were shaking."

He returns the bottle with the honey mixture to the backpack and settles back into position, wrapping his arms tightly around Carlos and Gonzalez's knees to avoid being dragged into the sea.

Raul and Gerardo do something similar, intertwining their arms while holding onto the raft. Everyone remains silent, scared, and shivering from the cold. This is hell, but instead of fire, it is made of water; the apocalyptic end of these men's dreams seems to have arrived. However, the crew remains calm, avoiding panic and despair at all costs and each hiding their fear.

The wind continues to howl, whipping the waves into a frenzy, and the raft creaks and groans under the strain. If the storm surge endangers the structure, they will have no choice but to jump into the water and cling to the raft's sides until the storm ends. Even on land, they had discussed this possibility as a last resort, as a desperate measure to save Esperanza and themselves. They hold on tight, but hope fades as the storm rages on. The possibility of jumping into the water looms large in their minds, a looming threat they must be ready to face at any moment.

The situation is dire. They are powerless against the fury of nature and are at the mercy of the elements. Death's face has never been so close. It is the time when even the most skeptical person grasps for something to cling to, some hope of survival. In this moment of fear and desperation, they call out to a higher power, seeking solace and protection. The reality of their mortality is all too clear, and the power of nature is a humbling reminder of their smallness in the vast, menacing ocean.

Roberto breaks the silence calm but worriedly, asking his friend to pray. "Raul, ask your people to help us."

"That's what I'm doing. I have faith in these people and know they will not fail me," Raul says. In his peculiar way of praying, Raul addresses his deities as close friends or acquaintances.

Raul and his cousin, Gonzalez, stand out for their devotion among the crew members. They have brought replicas of the Virgin of Regla and Saint Lazarus along with them. Both deities hold special significance for them.

The Virgin of Regla, known as the 'Queen of the Seas,' is the patron saint of sailors and fishermen. She offers protection and guidance on the treacherous waters. Saint Lazarus, also referred to as the miraculous, is revered for his healing miracles and his power to open ways, remove obstacles, and grant favors. As firm believers, Raul and Gonzalez hope these figures will provide protection and guidance during their journey.

"God..." Roberto invokes a silent prayer. "If you're really up there, you know I haven't been a man of faith, but you also know I've done no one wrong. Lord," the young man pauses as he takes a deep breath, "today I need you. Please, give me a hand."

Despite his lack of faith, Roberto feels a sudden and inexplicable sense of calm wash over him as he concludes his prayer, as if something, or someone, has heard him.

Midnight has long passed. Although strong, the wind has remained steady for the last few hours; wind gusts are not punching the crew with the same intensity as before. It seems like the storm peak is over. The surge did not reach the critical levels the crew feared, so no one needed to jump into the water. The cold is becoming a significant issue, but for Roberto, his major concern is in which direction they are being swept away by the storm.

The young navigator grips the compass tightly, his hands trembling as he studies it closely. Thankfully, the wind is blowing to the northwest, a direction which keeps them on course, preventing the expedition from being pushed off track.

"Good! I hope the wind doesn't change direction," he thinks, a sense of relief in his mind.

The crew is exhausted. The stress had not allowed them to have a decent night's rest for days before their departure. They haven't laid down on a bed for over thirty-six hours. Their eyelids weigh down like cobblestones. Despite the biting cold and the incessant rocking of the waves, they can't help but succumb to brief moments of slumber. During these frequent sleep nods, dangerous hallucinations lurk and sweep through their minds.

The water looks cloudy as if the raft is dragging dirt. Roberto thinks, "the coast must be nearby."

From his readings on Florida's geography, he knows a large part of the southern coast is swampy. This idea in his subconscious added to the ash-red color the sea has taken on as a reflection of the sky, feeds the young man's imagination.

"Let's see if I can reach the bottom," Roberto thinks, his semi-hypnotic state obscuring his reasoning.

"Don't! Don't do it!" a voice from within stops him. "Don't be a fool. Can't you see it's too soon?"

According to his calculations, with no setbacks, they should arrive three or four days after launching. But they have only been sailing for roughly twenty-eight hours. At that moment, Roberto loses his balance, and his foot slips through the hole in one of the inner tubes at the raft's base.

"No!" Roberto wakes up terrified, jerking his leg out of the water. "I was dreaming," he thinks, breathing a sigh of relief. And as his awareness awakes, a scary thought storms through him. "Was I dreaming or hallucinating? I don't know if I was asleep. Am I losing my mind?" he wonders. Many rafters have disappeared after jumping into the water because of hallucinations.

It's almost two in the morning. The intensity of the wind has decreased, and the sea has calmed down, although not completely. Isolated waves still threaten the expedition, though they no longer shake the boat as savagely.

The sky has lost its ash-red hue and turned dark, showing the storm has passed. However, the five men remain huddled, weak, overcome by sleep, and curled up like caterpillars to keep warm from the unbearable cold.

"I don't want you to go!" Between sobs, Roberto's girlfriend's voice pulls him out of his detached state.

"Please, don't cry," he asks with empathy, his tone soft. "You know I don't want to leave, but I can't let them go alone. What will I do if they don't make it?"

Just as they are getting into the conversation, an unexpected external force abruptly breaks their focus.

"Don't go, I'm talking to you!" the young woman cries out angrily.

"I'm not leaving. I don't know what's going on! They're pushing me!" a massive wave jolts him back to reality.

"Watch out!" some crew members' voices ring out.

A towering wave hits the boat's front-right corner first and lifts the raft at a dangerous angle, catching the crew off guard.

"To the right!" Gerardo, the first to receive the wave's impact, shouts, and everyone rushes toward the starboard rail to counterweight.

The front right part of the raft rises above the liquid mountain's crest. For an instant, the boat's bow hangs suspended in the air, almost vertical, before plummeting toward the deep abyss left in the wave's wake.

"To the left… now!" Gerardo shouts again, and the crew quickly reverses their positions, transferring their weight to the port side.

The large inner tube in the bow takes the fall's impact. Thanks to its enormous size and sturdy bindings, the shock only makes a loud bang as the raft strikes the water's surface. The rubbery chamber has successfully absorbed the destructive energy of the crash.

"We almost capsized!" Raul says, alarmed.

"Bro, it caught us off guard," Gerardo says.

Carlos rubs his bleary eyes and declares, "Yeah, I think we were all asleep."

Sitting in a fetal position next to Roberto, Gonzalez remains silent, his limbs close to his torso and his head resting on his knees. Roberto elbows him, looking for any sign of a response.

"Are you okay?"

Gonzalez raises his head and loosens up his tight posture, showing the part of the stick he is gripping to his chest. "Me? Here, holding on to my oar."

Roberto pats Gonzalez on the shoulder in recognition of his determination.

The crew remains on high alert for a time, wary of another surprise wave. Water runs down their faces, their clothes are soaked, and their bodies are numb from the cold and humidity. But they refuse to give up. They keep their spirits steady and hope for a better tomorrow.

Time continues its stubborn and eternal march. As dawn breaks, a gentle breeze from the east seems to erase the traces of the raging stormy sea. The sky lightens, and the stars twinkle, signaling the clouds' retreat. Silence reigns.

"I think we could set up the sails," Carlos says, his voice low and slow, breaking the eerie silence.

"Yes, I agree," Gerardo adds.

"Alright!" Roberto rubs his hands in front of his face as he warms them with his breath. "Let's set the sails!"

With renewed energy, the crew sets to work, crawling from their hunched postures to their positions, but this time, they move slowly. Their exhaustion is palpable. The darkness and the vessel's gentle rocking act as sleeping drugs on the young men.

As they stretch their bodies, Roberto moves to the helmsman's position, from where he will control the mainsail. The team's navigator takes the compass hanging from his neck to set the course. He uncovers the small plastic cover protecting the housing with the magnetic needle.

"We have to turn the raft to the left," he says, studying the precious instrument.

"Where do I have to hit it?" Carlos asks as he adjusts the rear right oar.

"You row forward. And Raul, you take the front left oar and row backward," Roberto instructs.

The young men flap their oars. With little effort, Esperanza turns on herself, moving her bow from east to north.

"Yeah, that's good!" Roberto calls out. "Now, let's unfurl the sails!"

The crew unfurls the sails in an organized way, but they don't move as quickly as before. Their bodies shake; the cold has numbed their muscles, but their determination to see the journey through triumphs over the adversities.

Raul and Gerardo set and secure the small sail. Carlos unfurls the mainsail while Roberto pulls the guiding line, making the canvas slide along the boom. Finally, the sail reaches its maximum amplitude, and Roberto sets it at the correct angle. A gentle wind billows the rustic triangular canvas, and Esperanza sails peacefully.

The tip of the boom that holds the mainsail unfurled. Photo taken by Raul.

The waves (averaging 10 feet high) seemed insignificant in the presence of the two massive twin waves (about 15 feet high) that came every 20 minutes. Photo taken by Raul.

Carlos - compass in hand - verifies the course of the expedition while holding the rudder with his left hand. Photo taken by Raul.

7

A NEW DAY

Dawn breaks with a clear glow on the horizon. The crew watches eagerly, yearning for the sunrise more than ever before. Roberto realizes Gonzalez has been silent and still for a long time.

"Gonzalez!"

The man raises his head, picking under his cap's visor. "What?"

"Are you okay?"

"You told me not to let go," he says, letting Roberto see the rear end of the oar he still grips to his body.

Gonzalez had held onto the oar all night, his grip never once loosening, as if his life depended on it.

"You held it the whole night? Wow, man. That's impressive, but the danger has passed, at least for now," the young navigator says.

Gonzalez extracts the oar from the water and fastens it, tethering it to the side rail of the raft.

The sky turns to steel, and the first lights of dawn seem to emerge from the depths of the sea. After a terrible night, a beautiful day begins. The sun rises, casting golden beams of light toward infinity and dyeing the entire eastern portion of the sky with its golden ink. On their trajectory, some of these beams hit the clouds, turning them into a spectacle of incandescent colors. A radiant solar ring emerges beyond the horizon, where the distant sea seems to boil.

The five young rafters remain silent, stunned by such beauty. They have never seen such a spectacular sunrise. Perhaps because they have never yearned for dawn so much, or maybe because they thought they would never see it again.

Wednesday, May 26.

The gentle morning breeze swells the sails, propelling the expedition forward. The sleep-deprived crew check in with the helmsman on duty often to confirm their heading.

"Course?"

"North!" the helmsman on duty assures repeatedly, letting his friends know he is not asleep.

The crew is more animated, although sleep consumes them. They have not touched a bed since Monday's dawn, some forty-eight hours ago. It has been two days of intense labor and insomnia, interrupted by occasional snatches of sleep and moments of fear through the night.

Time passes slowly. To fight boredom, the five crew members sing songs and share jokes and personal anecdotes. However, Carlos can't shake off his anxiety.

"How is it we have seen no Key yet?"

Carlos listened to Radio Martí every day. He had heard news about the 'Brothers to the Rescue' pilots spotting Cuban rafters in Sal and Perro Keys.

Roberto gazes at his brother, offering a serene smile. Carlos has always been an active person. Even when they played hide and seek as kids, he could never stay still in one place.

"Be glad we have seen no Keys. Those Keys are much further east, off our route."

Roberto explains the rafters arriving on those Keys have fled from central Cuban provinces like Matanzas or Las Villas. In the worst cases, they left from Havana, but the Gulf Stream dragged them off course. He further adds that there is nothing but water between Havana and Key West.

Carlos's concern fades as he listens to his brother's explanation.

"Alright! You have studied the crossing, but I can't take another night."

Carlos's words hint at unease again, but Gerardo steps in.

"Bro, not just one night… whatever it takes! The goal is to get there," the crew's doctor says with energy. "If we don't spot land after four days, then we'll head west until we reach the coast of Florida, right?" Gerardo asks Roberto.

"Hm-hmm. If we don't see land in four days, we keep watching the Stream flow. If the current veers north, we'll be east of Florida, not south, because the sea current flows around the coast. In that case, we'll have to sail west."

Roberto has spent countless hours studying the treacherous Gulf Stream. He understands its origins, temperature, speed, and trajectory.

The Gulf Stream originates at the equator in the Atlantic Ocean, thanks to the Earth's rotation. Despite what some believe, its trajectory never shifts. Enormous masses of air moving in the opposite direction to the Earth's rotation push the surface of the ocean west, creating a surface sea current of extraordinary dimensions.

Upon reaching South America, these waters divide into two large torrents. One heads south, bordering Brazil, toward the chilly waters of the South Atlantic. The other torrent diverts north, heading to the Caribbean Sea. A significant part of this northward torrent enters the Gulf of Mexico through the Strait of Yucatan, south of Cuba.

As it exits the Gulf of Mexico through the Straits of Florida, the Gulf Stream becomes a powerful, deep current. The current then heads north along the east coast of the United States toward the North Atlantic.

Eventually, this ocean current becomes the North Atlantic Drift, moving east toward the Norwegian Sea. Upon reaching Europe, part of this stream joins the Canary Current, traveling south off the coasts of Europe and the northwest part of Africa. Finally, it reaches the Equatorial Atlantic to continue its never-ending journey once more.

This explains why rafts' remnants have often been found near the shores of Miami Beach, Pompano Beach, and, in some extreme cases, even near Cape Canaveral.

Noon arrives as the clock ticks. As on the previous day, the wind intensifies, pressing the expedition forward at a faster pace.

Gonzalez calls out to his friends. "Don't you guys feel hungry?"

"I think it's time we ate something," Gerardo agrees.

"What's the status of the provisions?" Roberto asks.

"We still have a gallon of fresh water we haven't touched and a two-liter bottle of water with sugar, honey, and lemon that's still unopened. And there's also some of the water and sugar mixture in the other bottle we've been using," Gerardo reports while going through the backpacks.

"And we have the large container of water and sugar," Raul adds.

"That's right!" Roberto says. "Let's use the water from the container and save the mixture with honey for the nights. We'll need it to fight off the cold."

Raul's gaze is drawn to the cumbersome container. The two-inch diameter hole at its center top poses an inescapable conundrum.

"How do we get the water out of the tank?"

Raul's inquiry hangs in the air, an unspoken challenge sparking a lively discussion, with each member contributing their unique perspective.

After moments of contemplation, the team decides to refill the two-liter bottle they've been relying on, yet they face a daunting obstacle. The tank's mouth is too small to dip the empty bottle inside, and the risky prospect of lifting the tank to pour its contents into the bottle looms over them. The raft's unpredictable movements could easily lead to a loss of balance, endangering the precious cargo.

Carlos, the group's most resourceful member, steps forward with a potential solution. "I can use my fisherman's knife to break open the top of the tank so we can dip the bottle inside," he says.

Carlos's proposal holds merit, but the prospect of damaging the container lingers as a haunting potential consequence. In the event of a capsize, they might find themselves without their primary food source. Roberto, who had remained silent for a few minutes, finally breaks his silence. He carefully weighs everyone's ideas and contemplates the possibilities. His revelation cuts through the tension.

"I've got it! We can use the hose from the air pump to siphon out the water and sugar and refill the bottle without jeopardizing the tank."

The suggestion, once uttered, carries a sense of relief and hope, providing a glimmer of a solution amid their precarious circumstances.

The air pump sits securely under the helmsman's seat, ready to be used as part of the repair kit in case an inner tube loses air pressure. In the worst-case scenario, if a tube sustains serious damage, the crew can quickly replace it with the spare tube. This is their backup plan to improve their chances of success.

They keep the spare tube ready and inflated. It's slightly smaller than the other four tubes, and they arranged it inside the internal hole of the large farm tractor's inner tube at the bow.

The crew agrees with Roberto's proposal. So far, there has been no need to use the air pump, and they can reinstall the hose if a tube mishap occurs.

Carlos unstraps the air pump and places it over the helmsman's seat while Roberto searches through the backpacks for the fisherman's knife. Instead, he finds an old table knife traveling in their luggage.

"This will work."

Roberto takes the knife and prepares to cut the hose. His brother holds the hose stretched.

"Cut it long enough to reach the tank's bottom," he says.

Once the operation is complete, Carlos ties the air pump under the helmsman seat so it doesn't get lost. As he secures the item, his brother rinses the hose with seawater. Roberto inserts one end of the hose into the tank's narrow opening while Carlos creates a suction on the opposite end of the makeshift water extractor. The priceless blend streams forth, and he promptly positions the hose's end into the empty bottle's aperture.

As soon as the bottle is full, Roberto lifts the end of the hose, interrupting the fluid, and the siblings proceed to cover the tank and bottle, respectively.

"It's done!" Roberto says, tucking the hose inside a backpack.

Gonzalez grabs the bottle, and, downing two big gulps of the sticky mixture, cries out. "Ahhhhh!" Then he passes it to his cousin.

His cousin eagerly takes the bottle from him and grimaces as he takes a sip.

"Shit! This is like syrup."

The sun's heat has made the mixture in the container even harder to swallow. Gerardo drinks and Roberto follows him. Roberto's face contorts with discomfort as he offers the bottle to his brother, but Carlos shakes his head.

"No way, I don't want it. My stomach feels..."

Before finishing, Carlos leans over the railing and retches. His brother almost grabs him by the arm, but Carlos recovers quickly, sitting up straight, showing his strength.

"Do you feel dizzy?" Gerardo asks.

"No. I have an upset stomach, but I don't want to drink that stuff. It's disgusting."

"Bro, maybe that's why you vomited because your stomach is empty," Gerardo says, offering his medical advice. "You haven't eaten in hours. We know this mixture tastes bad, but you have to drink it, or else fatigue will set in and make things even worse."

Finally, with a look of distaste on his face, Carlos reluctantly drinks some of the cloying liquid.

As they continue their journey, the sun descends, casting a warm glow over the sea.

Roberto scans the faces of his fellow travelers, looking for someone to engage in conversation. They need a source of distraction to avoid thinking about the inevitable, the impending nightfall.

"Got any cravings for food once we get there?"

"Ham and cheese sandwich. Probably a couple of them," Gerardo says. "I'm starving."

"I'll eat anything," Gonzalez jokes, showing off his voracious appetite.

"I'd go for a pizza and an ice cream," Roberto says, and his brother nods.

"Same here."

The expedition continues its journey. With its rhythmic and imperturbable march, time is dragging one more day behind it. The afternoon gets old, and the sun sets, going down to its hiding place. Soon, it'll be dark.

This has been a long and lonely day. They have seen no ships. The only company the crew has is a small fish which, since morning, has swum under the raft and the occasional seagull flying overhead. The ocean swell has increased, but the crew is used to it by now, and it goes almost unnoticed.

"Did you guys see that?" Gerardo asks, alarmed, interrupting the temporary calm. His companions react like springs.

"What?"

"I thought I saw some fins over there," Gerardo's finger points to the northwest.

The crew falls silent, and Carlos grips the harpoon tightly, preparing for the worst. They're all on the lookout, waiting for the next wave to lift the raft and give them a better view. For a few moments, everyone remains observant. They are ready to face the fearsome encounter; they have no alternative.

"Look, look... there they are!" Gerardo shouts again.

Sure enough, several fins break through the surface in a particular waving pattern that helps Carlos identify the animals.

"They're dolphins!" Carlos says with excitement. His words bring relief and cheer to his fellow travelers, whose breath had stopped for a few seconds. "And it seems they're coming this way."

The pod of dolphins approaches the raft, welcoming the five sailors.

"There's a bunch of them!" Gonzalez says with emotion while the curious animals surround the small boat.

A group of around a dozen Atlantic spotted dolphins frolics around the raft. The crew remains frozen and silent, awed by their presence. These friendly creatures bring a sense of company and security as if they've come to visit. An almost mystical serenity encompasses the emotional encounter, where communication transcends human language, rooted in life and radiating with hope.

"Raul, get the camera!" Roberto asks the group's photographer.

"No way! I don't feel like taking photos," Raul's face reflects his exhaustion. His face is gaunt, and his lips dry and cut. He has yet to fully recover from the dizziness and vomiting of the previous day.

"Okay, I'll do it," Roberto says as he crawls to retrieve the camera from the backpack.

Just then, the dolphins beat a sudden retreat, giving the sailors no time to capture their friendly encounter on camera. The crew watches in surprise as the herd heads straight north as if leading the way. Soon, the magnificent creatures disappear into the endless ocean. The expedition sails on, and the crew prepares to endure another night at sea. Their minds linger on the memory of those friendly beings, their gazes fix on the horizon, and their hope for tomorrow is unwavering.

Carlos in the seat of the forward rowers near the bow. Beneath him, the spare tire is located. In the background, the small sail. On the far left the mainsail with the mast. Far right, Gerardo's leg is partially visible, standing on the starboard rail. Photo taken by Raul.

8

A HECTIC NIGHT

The dolphins are long gone, and the sea has turned into a shimmering gold, mirroring the sunset hues in the western sky. Although the strong, southeasterly winds have caused the swell to rise, the young crew can't tear their gaze away from the breathtaking sight. The memory of the previous night's horror fills them with trepidation, and they long to linger in the sun's company.

The last glimmer of sunlight sinks below the horizon, signaling the day is over. A sinister shade engulfs the eastern sky, shrouding the celestial view and erasing the horizon in its wake.

To the west, distant lights reveal a ship's presence. Although the rafters notice it, they do not halt their progress. Instead, they stay on course, pressing on with their perilous journey.

As darkness swallows them, the previous night's memories come alive, and the men's anxiety grows as they brace themselves for what is coming. Gerardo stations himself at the bow, vigilant to warn of any incoming waves. Raul stands beside him, helping to maintain the raft's balance. Carlos and Gonzalez remain steadfast at the rear oars, while Roberto maintains control of the mainsail from the helm. With the benefit of their previous night's experience, they face the darkness with newfound confidence.

The young crew does not lose sight of the unknown vessel approaching from the west, but they continue sailing north and resist the temptation to alter their course. The distant vessel stands out against the black backdrop of the night sky. In this vast expanse of darkness, the ship is the only visible presence besides the stars.

A flicker of light atop the ship catches their attention. Gradually, the speck detaches itself from the vessel and ascends.

"A helicopter!" the group's navigator shouts, his heart leaping into his chest.

The crew watches in awe as the minuscule light grows closer and larger, hurtling toward them.

"And it's headed this way!" Gerardo says, his voice heavy with excitement.

"Have they seen us?" Gonzalez asks.

The question hangs in the air, and Carlos wastes no time asking his brother to signal the incoming aircraft.

"Grab the flashlight."

Quickly, Roberto removes the construction gloves protecting his hands while the safety cords attached to each glove's edge keep them suspended from his wrists. He unbuttons his shirt pocket and retrieves a small flashlight wrapped in a plastic bag to shield it from water damage. It is the same flashlight they employed the first night to erect the mast. With the plastic wrapping removed, Roberto gets set to emit a sequence of light flashes comprising three rapid, three prolonged, and three quick flashes: the universal SOS signal in Morse code, a skill he learned during his preparations.

He points the flashlight at the helicopter and engages its switch.

"It doesn't work!"

The previous storm surge had been devastating, and the plastic cover had not been able to prevent the salty water from damaging the flashlight.

"Check the lid; it might be loose," his brother says, his voice filled with desperation.

The young man tries to adjust the device but to no avail.

The sound of his mother's voice reverberates in Roberto's mind, reminding him of her insistence that they pack a pocket lighter for the trip. She suggested it would be a backup illumination source if needed. It was a disposable pocket lighter, completely out of butane fuel, yet Cubans had devised a means to refill them, another innovation to endure the crisis. Roberto knew Carmen was right, but the shop's employee needed time to refill the lighter with liquefied gas, asking the young man to return later to pick it up. It was during the morning rush, the day of their departure. The escape plan was already in motion, and waiting an hour was a luxury he couldn't afford.

The helicopter continues its flight at a low altitude, and if it maintains its trajectory, it will pass very close to the small boat.

The young navigator knows he needs to act fast. He stows away the damaged flashlight and moves to the center of the raft, climbing over the starboard rail to gain more height. Roberto grips onto the mast with one hand and opens the compass cover with the other. He exposes the small mirror and raises it over his head to reflect the helicopter's own light toward its pilot.

The aircraft approaches, almost directly in front of them. Roberto keeps signaling while battling the raging waves rocking the raft like a wild colt, refusing its rider's commands. His crewmates watch anxiously, ready to help should Roberto fall into the water.

Silent and restless, the group experiences a moment of anguish and despair, wanting to scream but knowing any scream would go unheard. They hold their breath, staring at the chopper as it passes in front of them and continues, leaving them behind.

"We were so close," Gonzalez says, his sorrow palpable.

Loneliness and emptiness engulf the young men. Their eyes remain locked on the distant aircraft as it flies toward the horizon. A sense of hopelessness overwhelms them as they listen to the helicopter's engine fading, realizing their chance for salvation is slipping away.

Roberto remains standing, still looking and listening intently. He closes the lid of the compass and hangs it around his neck. A glimmer of light in the distance catches his attention.

"I see lights over there."

The rest of the crew perk up at the news. To them, lights are a sign of hope, a small yet powerful reminder there is still a chance of survival.

"Lights? Where?"

"Look in the helicopter's direction," Roberto says, pointing at the aircraft. "There's a light further back and another one to the left."

"Are you sure?" Raul asks, his excitement clear.

"Yep, that's what I'm seeing."

Sure enough, two dim lights, miles apart, seem to float in the thick darkness. Both shine at the same height, which makes Roberto presume they define something stretching behind the horizon.

"I don't want to get my hopes up, but if those lights aren't boats, it could be Key West," the young navigator says, his grip firmly on the mast.

"Bro, get down here. You could fall," Gerardo suggests.

The minutes seem to drag on, and time moves at a glacial speed. The helicopter has long disappeared, and the ocean has been steadily rising, the sound of the waves filling the air.

The unending nightfall and motionless time magnify the crew's weariness. The phosphorescent lights, swirling in the black waters, add to the surreal atmosphere, plunging the crew members into a semi-hypnotic state.

"We haven't seen the lights again," Carlos says, his tone shaky and a little unclear.

"They were probably just boats," Roberto replies, his voice heavy with sleep.

"Are we on course?" Gerardo asks from the bow, checking on the helmsman.

"North!" Roberto responds, trying to read the compass through half-closed eyes. His fatigue is overpowering, and he can't keep them open no matter how hard he tries.

To the west, a warm, ethereal glow in the sky reveals a well-lit area beyond the horizon. Despite this, the crew stays on course, even though progress has become slower and more arduous. The wind has shifted direction, now blowing from almost directly ahead. Thus, Roberto has had to readjust the mainsail to maintain their trajectory.

Meanwhile, the swell has also altered its pattern, no longer assaulting them from the starboard side but striking the boat almost dead-on, hurling its bow skyward like a launch pad before slamming it down against the surface.

As the bow's observer, Gerardo is on the alert.

"Another one!" he shouts every time a wave approaches, but the night's pitch blackness renders the crew unable to see the wave until they can feel its powerful force rising beneath them.

"Raul!" Gerardo calls his partner when he notices he is nodding off.

"What?" Raul asks, his voice hazy from sleep.

"Bro, wake up, or we're gonna capsize!"

Raul struggles to keep his eyes open, but the overwhelming fatigue takes hold. Gerardo empathizes with Raul's plight; the constant episodes of dizziness and nausea have drained his already fragile body. Determined to protect his friend, Gerardo has an idea.

"Let's cross our arms," he suggests, looping his left arm behind Raul's right elbow. "When I tug, move with me."

"Okay," Raul mumbles, nodding.

This way, Gerardo can keep a watchful eye on the waves while staying connected with his friend.

Raul's exhaustion is clear in his heavy eyelids as he struggles to stay awake in the passing minutes. Gerardo attempts to wake him up by jabbing him with his elbow, yet it has no effect. Raul's body is unresponsive, on the brink of incapacity.

"Another one!" Gerardo shouts as he hauls his friend into a sitting position.

Raul, dazed and confused, recalls his partner's advice and summons the last dregs of his strength to give a sharp tug, jolting Gerardo from his spot. But in his haze, Raul doesn't realize he has pulled his friend in the exact opposite direction, causing him to lose his balance and fall on top of him, leaning almost all his weight toward the left part of the bow.

"Let me go!"

Gerardo's desperate cry echoes through the night, increasing Raul's confusion. He cannot understand what is happening, but his partner knows all too well what this error could mean.

The devastating wave strikes the right corner of the bow, causing it to rise. As the wave advances, the entire starboard side lifts out of the water, reaching a critical angle. Capsizing seems imminent.

"To the right, now!" Roberto's instinctive voice commands and the crew responds by leaning even harder on the starboard rail, halting its ascent and preventing a capsize.

Gerardo disengages from Raul and launches himself onto the raised section of the bow. The raft's weight shifts to the right at the exact moment the boat crests the wave and falls precipitously toward the void left behind by the liquid mountain.

"To the left, to the left!" Roberto shouts with force, and the crew rushes to change position, attempting to soften the inevitable fall.

With a booming sound, the raft crashes into the wave's trough ten feet below, and the thunderous impact of the tires against the water's surface jolts the entire expedition.

In the wake of the close call, an eerie silence takes over the crew.

The men exchange glances, their faces unreadable in the darkness, but they all understand how close they have just been to a fatal end. Everything happened in a flash, leaving them shaken. A gloomy thought takes over the crew's mind as they realize Esperanza has taken a major impact, and they all wonder if she'll survive.

"Let's check out the raft," Carlos says, a tone of urgency in his voice.

Unable to see, the men use their hands and feet to inspect the raft's integrity. Their hearts pound with fear and anxiety as they move around the structure, checking the joints with their hands, tugging on the ropes, and pushing and kicking the inner tubes. With every tug and push, they hold their breath, waiting for a sign of weakness, but to their relief, the raft seems to have held up against the impact.

"It's still in one piece. We're lucky," Carlos says.

The caution and robust attention taken during Esperanza's construction has, once again, averted the crew from disaster.

Gerardo pours out his frustrations on Raul. "See what you did? We almost flipped."

"Man, I can't take it anymore. Just let me go. I'm gonna lie down, and if I die, so be it," Raul says. His defeatist tone makes Gerardo even more agitated.

"Stop talking shit because I'm gonna knock that nonsense out of you."

The man's threatening tone prompts Roberto to intervene. "Hey, you two! What's going on over there?"

"This one's ready to quit."

"Well, get on with it. This is not the place for a fight," Roberto says, a hint of authority in his tone.

"Don't worry, that's not gonna happen," Gerardo says.

A faint light that has been lingering in the sky for some time has grown brighter, warning of the impending presence of something large.

"Should we go off course and see what it is? It could be a Key," Roberto suggests.

"I don't think so," Raul, looking better, says. "Let's keep going. That's what we agreed on."

"Yeah, let's keep going," concedes the young navigator.

After all, Raul is right. Many rafters spend entire days drifting, trying to find help. The pursuit of such a search has resulted in an unfortunate number of casualties.

"There it is!" Carlos alerts.

The first glints of light emerge over the horizon's edge. Soon after, a radiant ship appears in view.

As time marches, the ship grows larger, continuing its approach at an impressive speed, its dazzling lights illuminating the dark expanse of water. If it maintains its course, it will come close to the expedition.

"It looks like the first one we saw," Carlos says.

Indeed, a beautiful cruise ship glimmers like a beacon in the dark ocean. Roberto's eyes are fixed on the distant vessel, lost in thought as he contemplates a dream.

"You guys think we could catch it?" Roberto asks with a hint of hope in his voice.

"Bro, those ships seem slow, but they are not," Gerardo reminds him.

"I know, and the issue is not only catching it but figuring out how to get onboard if they don't see us," Roberto says.

The young man comprehends that to board a ship on the high seas, they need the help of its crew. But the obscurity will make it impossible for the ship's passengers to detect them.

The men remain silent, watching the massive ship approaching from the southwest.

About half an hour later, the strange vessel gets closer, and Roberto's confusion grows as its direction of approach shifts from southwest to south.

"This can't be. We spotted the glow in the west. Next thing we knew, the ship appeared in the southwest, and now it's in the south. Did we leave it behind? No way can this raft move faster than a ship."

The fledgling navigator is plagued by queries, but as exhaustion impairs his cognitive abilities, he cannot discern a logical reason for this occurrence. Also, the wind, now blowing head-on and opposing the expedition's progress, continues to burden his mind.

As the ship draws nearer, roughly a mile from the expedition, it makes a slight turn to the left.

The navigator does not understand why he feels so attracted to this ship. He's drawn to it, sensing there's more to it than meets the eye, but he can't quite grasp what that is. "Guys, let's catch that ship!"

"There's no way we'll get it!" Raul says.

"Probably not, but we gotta do something because we are not making any progress," Roberto senses something isn't right.

"That's true," Carlos agrees. "The headwind is preventing us from moving forward."

"Bro, if we're gonna do it, let's do it now," Gerardo says.

For a moment, the crew remained silent, all eyes on Roberto, the only noise being the lapping of the waves against the raft.

"Let's do it!"

The navigator's command makes the crew spring into action. As Roberto loosens the rope holding the mainsail open, the sound of the canvas tugging against the mast echoes in the night.

"Carlos, pull in the sail and hold it until I tell you," Roberto instructs his brother.

Carlos kneels by the mast, his hands pulling the canvas in a steady, rhythmic motion as he retracts the mainsail. "Done!"

"Gerardo, shift the small sail to the right and keep it there."

The young man pulls the jib's boom over the starboard rail, forcing the small sail flat to the wind, and the raft turns left. As the boat approaches a 90-degree rotation, Roberto pulls the tension rope, unfurling the canvas while shouting to his brother.

"Release the sail!"

As the mainsail unfurls, the wind swells the stretched canvas, causing Esperanza to pivot as she completes a full 180° turn and is then propelled forward with force. Now blowing from behind, the wind propels the raft to an incredible speed, surprising even the young navigator. Despite his thorough study of sailing, Roberto has never been on a boat before, and the velocity and maneuverability of the vessel stun him. He shouts to the two crew members at the bow.

"Secure the small sail in there."

Throughout their voyage, they aligned the jib parallel to the mainsail to mitigate the turbulence the wind creates behind it. This occurs when the boat's path and the wind travel in different directions. But with the wind now blowing in their direction, the young sailor is determined to seize the opportunity.

Gerardo and Raul position the jib, catching the wind on the boat's right side. Meanwhile, the mainsail spans seven feet from the mast to the left, its massive size causing the wind force to press more heavily upon it and causing the vessel to tilt to the left. As Roberto secures the line stretching the mainsail, he keeps commanding the crew.

"Everyone, move to the right to counterbalance."

With swift resolve, Carlos, Raul, and Gerardo shift their weight to the starboard rail, anchoring their feet to the raft's lower structures. Roberto also moves to the right edge of the rudder's seat while Gonzalez, paralyzed by fear, remains in place, observing his crewmates' actions.

"Gonzalez, get over here!" Gerardo says with authority.

Gonzalez hesitates. His voice betrays a sense of fear. "There?"

"Yes, over here!"

"Do I have to sit on the railing?"

"Here, Gonzalez, here!" his partner insists, the urgency in his tone clear.

Gonzalez crawls, his movements slow and uncertain as he inches toward his new position. After what seems like an eternity, Gonzalez finally sits on the railing, gripping it tightly with his hands to steady himself against the wind and the boat's swaying.

Although most weight is concentrated on it, the raft's right side rises, gliding over the water's surface and occasionally losing contact with it. Meanwhile, the left side cuts through waves like a torpedo, picking up speed with each passing moment.

"Don't look down," Gonzalez says, his voice shaking and his eyes wide with fear.

"Why not?" Gerardo asks.

"Those glowing things."

The water flows between the raft's tires, forming whirlpools, and the tiny, green phosphorescent lights appear to stretch out, creating luminous circular beams, crazily twisting and turning in the dark ocean.

As the boat gains speed, the ropes securing the mast vibrate like guitar strings under the pressure of the wind pushing against both sails. With each wave working as a launching ramp, the raft seems to take off.

"We're going full sail ahead!" the team's navigator shouts with unrestrained joy, his eyes shining with excitement.

"Whoa, this is way too much! She's gonna break!" Carlos voices his concern, feeling the stress on the mainsail and the tensors holding the mast.

"She can handle it," Roberto says, assuring his brother, although he knows some ropes securing the tires are of poor quality.

The sudden rush of adrenaline caused by the abrupt shift in direction and speed invigorates the young crew, making them forget their fatigue.

Roberto uncovers the compass to determine their new heading and calculate the deviation from their route. But as he reads the startling result, he can't help but doubt the instrument's accuracy. "What? This cannot be!" he thinks, staring incredulously at the device.

Turning to the night sky, the man searches for an ancient navigation method: the stars. Fortunately, the sky is clear, dotted with twinkling stars, a vast improvement from the previous night.

"That's the Big Dipper, and further over there, the North Star. So, the compass is fine," he thinks.

Like a divine revelation, the fog of confusion lifts, and everything becomes clear to Roberto. The questions that have been swirling in his mind are at last answered. For the last couple of hours, they have been veering off course, their path gradually shifting to the right in a barely noticeable U-turn. This explains the ship's strange movements. The reality is that the ship appeared in the northwest and is now heading north, perhaps toward Florida.

"Guys, we're back on course!"

His fellow crewmates are confused for a moment, thinking they have gone off course pursuing the cruise ship. "What do you mean?"

The expedition's navigator clarifies the situation, shouting out in excitement, and the crew is filled with renewed hope and optimism, even though they know it's unlikely they'll catch up with the retreating luxury liner.

The sea, although less dangerous here, never remains calm. Photo taken by Raul.

Carlos, holding the compass, checks the expedition's course while steering with his left hand. To his left, the backstay line supporting the mast and the mainsail. Photo taken by Raul.

9

THE RETURN TO LIFE

A light drizzle reinforces the early morning coldness, deepening the exhausted crew's misery. A dense, gloomy silence hangs in the air, broken only by the occasional roar of the sea, like a beast rousing from its slumber.

Gerardo has taken over the helm, relieving the weary navigator who needs to rest. After a brief nap, Roberto lifts his head and removes the raincoat cap, shielding his face from the cold. He surveys the men. They are all silent, overcome by exhaustion and shivering and huddling together for warmth. He tallies up the number of crew members, including himself, and arrives at four.

"Where is Carlos?" he thinks.

Panic seizes the young navigator as he realizes Carlos is nowhere in sight. The thought of losing his brother sends shivers down his spine. He knows most cases of rafters being lost at sea occur at night.

And the most terrible fear makes him recover from his sleepy state. In desperation, Roberto scans his surroundings, searching for any sign of Carlos. A bulge in the sail's canvas, close to the mast, gives away his brother's presence, where he is seeking refuge from the windy rain.

"Thank God." Roberto takes a deep breath of relief as a peaceful smile grows on his face. Then, he swivels and covers his head with his raincoat's hood.

A bleak dawn breaks with a completely cloudy sky and no sun in sight. Although the rain has stopped, the gray clouds dominate the new day, casting a somber mood over the sea, which is now dressed in a wintry ashen color. The sun, trapped behind the foamy aerial barrier, is a mere opaque silhouette.

The crew is quiet, their spirits reflecting the gloomy morning. They yearn for a fleeting ray of sunlight to warm their soaked bodies, but in this weather, their hope feels distant. They know it's unlikely a 'Brothers-to-the-Rescue' airplane will find them in these conditions. No one would fly a plane in this weather. However, none of them voices their concerns.

The expedition persists, yet at a much slower pace than during the night, as the wind has significantly abated.

Time continues its unbreakable path. About three hours have passed since dawn. To the northern horizon, a thin, blue band stretches through the sky, signaling the end of the extensive cloud cover. Several miles to the southeast, a merchant ship glides through the choppy waves, heading north.

"That ship is too far away," Gerardo says.

"Hm-hmm," Roberto nods, observing the distant merchant liner.

The remaining crew show little interest in the vessel since it's traveling far away.

The ship continues its route northward and, eventually, sails parallel to the battered expedition, some miles to the east. In silence, the men watch their immense neighbor. Their visages reveal emotions of yearning, trepidation, and even a trace of desperation, particularly Gonzalez. One of his gloves slips from his hand and falls into the sea. To his companions' surprise, the young man stands still, his gaze fixed on the glove as it slowly sinks.

"Pick it up!" Raul's commanding voice wakes his cousin out of his trance.

In a swift move, Gonzalez drops forward and plunges his right arm into the water, retrieving the glove that was drifting away.

The seemingly negligible incident is the first sign of surrender exhibited by a crew member. However, it is also a testament to Raul's determination and resilience. Despite being the weakest man onboard, Raul still clings to his faith and stays resolute in his conviction that they will emerge victorious.

After retrieving the glove, Gonzalez heads back to the raft's stern and lies down. He reclines in the starboard corner and lowers his cap's visor to his eyebrows. Staring at his soaked, tattered tennis shoes and wrapping his arms around his torso, Gonzalez retreats into his own thoughts.

"Gonzalez, what's the matter?" Gerardo asks.

"I'm screwed." There is a helpless tone in his voice.

"Bro, that's bullshit. You're fine." His friend tries to encourage him, dismissing his feelings as nonsense, not wanting to see him as a defeated man, ready to give up the fight.

Gonzalez's reaction does not surprise his companions. They comprehend the mission is exceedingly difficult and that he joined the crew with barely any time to prepare. Therefore, embracing a passive demeanor has been the preferable alternative. In these circumstances, the person in distress can become unhinged and ignite disputes, often leading to tragedy.

The weather keeps improving, but the sea remains choppy, evidenced by the raft's continuous bouncing. The crew's positivity swells as a streak of sky blue pushes the grey clouds aside over the northern skyline.

A new mystery confronts the young navigator.

For the last few hours, Roberto has seen an unevenness to the horizon, as if it was not completely straight but instead tilted to the left.

"It can't be! Must be the fatigue," the man thinks as he migrates to the stern to take back control of the ship.

"Gerardo, get some rest. I'll take the rudder."

Gerardo readies himself to vacate his position as he entrusts the compass to his replacement.

"I don't really get it, but it looks like the ocean is leaning that way. Am I hallucinating?" astounded, Gerardo asks Roberto, sketching an angled line with his arm to illustrate the degree.

"Nah, I'm seeing the same. Must be exhaustion; nothing else it could be."

For a moment, they both look out at the skyline but refrain from attaching any significance to the illusion. They understand it is a figment of their imaginations. In reality, the constant pounding of waves on the boat's right side has caused the crewmates to lean unconsciously in that direction.

Almost an hour has passed since they lost sight of the freighter, and the men's eyes strain to pick out any sign of salvation on the vast expanse of the sea. Another ship emerges from the northwestern skyline, bringing a fresh ray of optimism to the crew.

"Look! There goes another one," Carlos says, pointing toward the distant speck.

Gerardo gazes into the distance, shielding his eyes from the brightness.

"Yeah, but it's way further off than the last one."

"It's heading east," the group's navigator says while examining the voyager's path.

Meanwhile, Raul ties a small replica of La Virgen de Regla to the raft's bow, asking her to calm the fury of the sea. He also prays to Saint Lazarus 'the Miraculous' for the strength to endure their agonizing odyssey.

The merchant has been traveling along the skyline. As it passes in front of the expedition, it makes a sharp turn left, following the same course as the raft.

"It's turning north," Roberto says, watching as the ship is subsumed by the unattainable horizon.

It's past ten in the morning when the second freighter disappears, intensifying the crew's feeling of isolation. A sense of solitude lingers in the air, occasionally broken by a seagull. But as time passes, a new gray dot emerges toward the northwest, heading in the same direction as the previous traveler.

"Another one!" Roberto shouts from the helm, his eyes fixed on the remote vessel.

Carlos turns around, his excitement palpable. "Where?"

"There, where the other came from," the navigator says, his finger pointing to the northwest.

"Bro, I thought today was gonna be a boring day," Gerardo says, referring to the adverse weather they faced at dawn.

The crew is more animated. The presence of a ship for the third time that morning represents not only a visual contact with the world but also a glimmer of hope for the expedition members.

Roberto watches, shocked, as Raul breaks apart the plaster image of Saint Lazarus.

"What are you doing?"

"A wise old woman told me if things get ugly, I must pray, break the image, and throw a piece into the water."

"Okay, you know better than me," Roberto says, a look of incomprehension on his face.

A while later, the crew watches as the dot on the horizon grows larger, reminding them of an old acquaintance from the past.

"It's a tourist cruise," Carlos says. "Like the one from the first day."

They all stare at the distant ship, enchanted by its beauty. Carlos is right; it is a magnificent cruise liner similar to the one they encountered a few miles from Havana.

"If it's not the same ship, it looks identical," Roberto says.

"And it's not going to Mexico," Raul's statement shows his intention to board the ship if this one stops.

Roberto gets his friend's message. His heart beats faster as he contemplates the possibility of being rescued. He knows the odds are against them, but he also knows hope is the only thing keeping them going. The man takes a deep breath and gazes at the ship. Hoping its crew will see them and come to their rescue, he opens the compass to employ its mirror in the same way he did the night before with the helicopter.

The cruiser sails eastward, closing its distance from the battered raft. Everything shows it will pass about six miles in front of the expedition, far enough for the small boat to get lost in the vast expanse of the ocean. Despite the improved weather, the waves still reach over eight feet, making it highly unlikely for the expedition to be spotted from so far away.

Roberto positions himself at the raft's center as the massive cruiser approaches its closest point. Like in the night, he climbs over the starboard side rail and grasps onto the mast, compass in hand. He opens the instrument's lid and raises his arm, directing the circular mirror toward the ship. The man hopes for a lucky light flash to reach the pupils of a passenger on deck.

After a while, his efforts appear fruitless, and Roberto lowers his arm.

"Too far… they can't see us."

"Keep trying!" Raul says.

"Of course, but my arm already hurts."

As the waves lift the raft, Roberto seizes the opportunity to signal from the highest viable location. He stands next to the mast, observing the approaching luxury liner with keen eyes, ready to send signals at any moment. With each lift of the waves, he sends a flash of light toward the distant ship, hoping to catch someone's attention.

The cruise liner maintains its course, and as it passes in front of the expedition, it turns left, following the same trajectory as the previous freighter. Disappointed, the rafters watch as the ocean liner veers away, knowing their chances of being rescued are dwindling with each passing moment.

"It's turning away. They didn't see us," Carlos says, a dreadful tone in his voice.

Once again, a hush descends upon the crew as they watch the cruise leave them behind. The massive vessel sails north, following the same route as the expedition but several miles ahead of it.

"We're right on track!" Roberto's voice cut through the stillness, sounding strong and confident. His sudden outburst creates a spontaneous confusion among his fellow travelers.

"We've been going north... right?" Gerardo asks, confused.

"Yeah, but we weren't sure how far the current was dragging us," Roberto adds.

"Looks like we're alright. We sail north if the current moves east. And if the current shifts north, it'd mean we'll already be sailing east of Florida, so we'd have to sail west. Am I right?" Gerardo recites from memory what they planned after studying the Gulf Stream.

"You're right, but did you see those three ships? Notice their courses? The first went straight north. The other two were heading east and turned north in front of us. Don't you see why?" The navigator's hints help his friend understand.

"Bro...! They're heading to Florida. The last two boats had to go around the Keys," Gerardo's conclusions coincide with his partner's.

"Exactly! The Florida Keys must be a few miles behind that ship."

Leaving a trail of churning waves in its wake, the magnificent liner continues, moving further away from the raft. With their spirits restored, the young crew watches the symbolic messenger with awe as it disappears beyond the horizon.

The gray cloud barrier has retreated to the southern sky. By comparison, the northern firmament displays an immense azure backdrop embellished with billowy white cumulus clouds. The expedition presses on, and the crew buzz with energy, all except Gonzalez, who sits still and quiet in the stern.

"Hey Gonzalez, what's going on?" Gerardo asks in a lighthearted tone.

"I'm screwed up!" The young man gives the same answer he had voiced hours before. His face wears the expression of someone resigned to his fate, and his eyes hold the knowledge of his impending death.

"C'mon, bro, you are not giving up now, are you?" Gerardo asks, yet Gonzalez remains indifferent to his friend's pleas.

The sun makes its way toward the top of the sky, announcing that noon is arriving. More than an hour has passed since the luxurious ship faded from their view. The crew is desperate to reach the elusive horizon, hoping it will soon stop running ahead of them. Everyone is trying to find something to occupy their time, except for Gonzalez, who remains lying down.

"Let's see what food we have left," Roberto says, disrupting the inertia.

"The sugar water tank is almost full, and the honey bottle's got a liter in it," Gerardo says.

"What about the gallon of fresh water we got?" the navigator asks.

"That one's still untouched. I gave Raul a sip when he was vomiting."

"We'll keep that gallon in case of emergencies," Roberto says while assessing the cargo at the stern. "Guys! There's a tube out of place back here."

The wild, tumultuous seas and the incredible speed achieved by the raft the night before had caused the stern's left inner tube to shift a few inches out of place. Roberto leaves his post to go fix it.

"Gonna see if I can squeeze it in," the young man announces as he climbs over the railing, venturing beyond the safety zone.

Holding onto the wooden rail with both hands, Roberto jumps on the misaligned airlock tube. With every bounce, the tire gives a slight jolt and moves back about an inch.

"Be careful not to fall," Gerardo says.

After several attempts, the tube slides to its rightful spot. Roberto adjusts the ropes holding the tire in place before returning to the safety area.

"Hey, somebody pass me an oar," Carlos, sitting in the bow, asks the men at the stern.

Carlos has settled himself in the front rowers' seat and has prepped the port oar to use it.

"What are you doing?" his brother asks.

"I'm gonna row to get my mind off things," Carlos says.

"It's better to save energy. Rowing won't make the raft go faster."

"I get it, but I'm not as patient as you, and it makes me nuts being stuck here not doing anything." Carlos refers to his brother's ability to stay still for hours.

Roberto knows conserving energy is essential, but remaining composed and cool-headed is even more important. Thus, he supports Carlos's judicious decision and unties the oar, passing it over to his brother.

Carlos positions the rustic instrument, knotting the strings to ensure it won't get lost if it falls into the sea. The young man pulls on the oars, and the splashes of water accompany his strong, regular strokes.

As Carlos rows, his gaze locks on the distant southern horizon behind which Cuba stretches. Roberto observes him from the helm and notes a mix of sadness and determination in Carlos's eyes. Roberto can't help but remember his brother sitting on the raft back in the attic, lost in thought.

"Thinking of your son?"

Carlos nods, his eyes still full of moisture as he stares out at the southern ocean boundary.

"He's probably looking for me all over right now..." His lips twist, and a knot in his throat stops him from finishing his sentence.

Roberto turns around and faces south, sharing his brother's anguish; he frequented Carlos's house and loved playing with his little nephew.

Time marches on, and it's already noon. The young navigator continues to scan the horizon, not realizing that sometimes the landscape blurs before his eyes. A wave crashes against the raft, jolting him awake from his drowsiness.

Roberto's gaze sweeps the scene, taking in the crew before settling on Esperanza. His left hand gently runs along the rough surface of the wooden structure, marveling at how well she has held up.

"You've been so good!" Roberto reflects. "I'll miss you when this is all over."

After his silent confession, the group's navigator looks toward the northeast, a light breeze brushing against the back of his head. The mainsail casts a shadow on his left view. His overwhelming exhaustion and longing to see dry land prompts his mind to discern the remarkable image of a farmhouse behind the sail's outline.

"A house?" Roberto cranes his neck forward and is about to stand to get a better look behind the mainsail when his conscience's voice rings in his head, urging him to stop.

"Wait! How can a house be in the middle of the sea? Am I losing it?" The man sits in silence, deep in thought, as he worries about his mental state. "No way. I need some sleep."

Roberto contemplates telling Gerardo about the situation but stalls in his decision. He doesn't want to alarm his friend.

"Gerardo, take over for a while. I need to rest."

"Sure, you look exhausted."

"Just keep us on course."

"Got it," Gerardo says as he moves to occupy the helmsman's position.

The young navigator hands the compass to his friend and abandons the rudder, moving to the center of the raft. He sits at the boat's lowest section, atop the inner tubes, with just a few inches of air between him and the sea's surface. Resting his back against the mast's base, the man extends his feet toward the stern and closes his eyes, covering his face with his hat. Although the water constantly bathes him from the waist down, his exhaustion is such that he falls asleep almost instantly.

"Look who showed up!" A group of people in a lighted room laugh and celebrate Roberto's arrival. Roberto looks around and sees his loved ones and hometown friends, including his former classmates, with whom he has shared the last four years of his life.

"What are you guys doing here?" Roberto asks, surprised by the unexpected reception.

"Looking forward to hearing from you," Carmen, his mother, answers with a warm, maternal inflection in her voice.

"We're alright, we keep going," the man says.

"What about the others? Aren't they coming?" a voice from the group cuts in.

"The others? They're fine! I'm waiting for them to wake me up." A brief silence follows his response, showing the navigator's confusion.

The image of the bright room turns blurry as the people fade away, replacing the man's dream with his reality: a vast and unforgiving ocean. Roberto's eyes open, and he finds himself back on the raft, shivering with his body drenched. He blinks and rubs his eyes, trying to shake off the illusion.

He looks around and sees his friends at their posts, carrying out their duties. The sun is still high in the sky, casting a blinding light on the endless blue water. Roberto exhales a deep breath and feels his heart racing.

"It was just a dream," he thinks, "a cruel trick of my mind."

Roberto adjusts his hat and glances at his feet, his tennis shoes and pans soaked in salt water. He then looks down; an intense dark blue reminds him of the ocean's infinite depth. He closes his eyes and pulls down his hat, trying to drift back to sleep, when an unexpected wave washes over his torso, forcing him to sit up.

The young navigator pulls his hat back and lets it hang from his neck. The bright sunlight forces him to squint as he looks up at the sky. Closing his eyes, he takes a deep breath of salty air and feels the sun's heat warming his face. He peels back his heavy eyelids. The brightness bothers him, but he bears it. He looks around, surveying the rustic wooden structure and the inner tubes beneath him. He glances at Gonzalez, who remains motionless in the same spot. With his left foot, Roberto taps his friend's leg to check if he is okay. Gonzalez responds by tilting his head back and letting out a fleeting glance from under his cap's visor. Gonzalez is the only crew member wearing a cap. Finally, the group's navigator prepares to return to his post as he stretches his arms and adjusts his hat, looking out at the vast ocean. The endless blue horizon stretches out before him, and he feels insignificant in comparison.

A distant bird flying close to the surface of the sea catches the navigator's attention.

"Another seagull," he thinks.

Roberto's eyes follow the bird's flight, mesmerized by the effortless glide and freedom it represents. The bird flies toward them, and soon, its wings intrigue the man; they are outstretched and static, not flapping at all.

"Is my mind playing tricks on me? No, no, I'm awake," he whispers to himself as he climbs to his feet.

"A plane! Look, a plane!" the young navigator screams, pointing at the distant airplane, a high pitch and sense of excitement in his voice. "And it's coming this way!"

The news erupts like thunder, breaking the silence and causing the rest of the crew to turn around in shock at the incredible announcement. Sure enough, a small Cessna Skymaster is approaching from the south, and the faint roar of its engines gets louder as it draws closer. What had been a serene atmosphere is now bustling with commotion. Gonzalez gets up and sits next to the helmsman's seat, joining his friends in celebration, a wide grin spread across his face. Overcome with joy, the young sailors shout and laugh with euphoria, tears streaming down their faces. They wave their arms in the air to greet the aircraft's crew, who bring them news of life.

"Bro, I'm crying," Gerardo tells Carlos.

"Me too," Carlos replies as he lifts the oars.

Raul and Roberto share a triumphant high five, their palms pressing together with a satisfying squeeze.

"We made it!" Raul says, his voice unsteady, breaking with emotion.

His friend nods in silence, the smile on his face transcending words; the excitement is immense.

It's 12:45 p.m. on Thursday, May 27, as the expedition embarks on the last leg of its journey: the return to life.

The plane flies dangerously low over the raft, its engines roaring loudly. As it passes, the two-engine aircraft turns left and circles the area at about twenty-five feet above sea level. Through its small hatches, the rafters can see its occupants' faces as they wave their arms, greeting the young sailors.

"Hey, gimme the camera!" Raul asks Roberto.

In a hurry, Roberto retrieves the instrument from Raul's backpack, unwraps it, and hands it to the eager photographer, who begins snapping away.

After circling the raft twice, the copilot opens his window and throws an item out as the plane passes right over the vessel.

"Look, look, they threw something!" Gonzalez shouts.

The object lands in the water, bobbing about twenty yards from the boat. It is a half-gallon jug made of white plastic with a red cap and a large 'Brothers-to-the-Rescue' sticker plastered on it.

"It's a pitcher," Carlos and Gerardo declare in unison.

The copilot dropped the receptacle west of the expedition, anticipating the current would carry it toward the raft. However, the plane's crew had not realized this raft sails faster than similar vessels they had encountered before. Realizing they will leave the jug behind, the young sailors decide to halt their progress.

"Let's get it!" Roberto shouts as he releases the guide rope that holds the mainsail taut, causing the sail to billow in the wind.

Gerardo, kneeling next to the mast, picks up the canvas. The raft gradually loses speed until it stops. Carlos sets the front oars and starts rowing in reverse, his oars' blades cutting through the water and making Esperanza move backward.

The jug draws closer to the left side of the boat, and the crew prepares to intercept it. Gerardo leans over the rail, his upper body suspended over the surface as he stretches his arm and catches the container.

"There's a message in here!" the man says excitedly as he pulls off the cap and extracts a rolled sheet of paper from within.

"What's it say?" his companions ask, their eyes wide with apprehension.

"Welcome to the land of freedom," Gerardo reads. "The US Coast Guard is coming your way. God is with you. Brothers to the Rescue."

The young sailors beam with joy as they unfurl the mainsail once again, its fabric flapping in the wind until fully swollen. As the raft gains momentum, two other planes approach the scene, and the men at sea continue to wave and greet their new friends in the air.

"Three of them now!" they shout.

"I'm out of film already," Raul says. "I'm gonna hide the film so I won't lose the photos if the Coast Guard takes my camera away."

"Right! Do it now!" Roberto agrees.

Those unfamiliar with communist governments may view the photographer's reaction as odd. However, to these men, raised in the constant presence of censorship and surveillance, it is a logical decision.

"Make sure it doesn't get wet," Roberto says.

Raul extracts the delicate film from the camera, wraps it in a plastic bag, and slides it into his shirt pocket. Next, he conceals his camera in his backpack.

After circling the area for several minutes, two of the planes move off, leaving one behind, hovering above. Its crew releases a second container, and the sailors below hear the thud as it hits the water.

"They threw another one!" Gerardo says.

This time, the pilots improve their aim, so the rafters don't need to stop the boat. However, Carlos vigorously rows backward to slow the raft's momentum.

The jug is on track to pass behind the stern. Roberto reacts quickly, leaning over the last tire's edge, his left hand gripping the rubber while his right hand reaches out for the container. He snatches the drifting object and passes it to Gonzalez, who steadies Roberto's leg with a firm grip before pulling the man back into the raft's safety.

This new container is like the previous one, although smaller, about half the size.

Gonzalez unscrews the jug's lid and peeks inside. A dark liquid sparkles, its coolness transferring through the plastic to Gonzalez's hands. The man sniffs the contents as a deliciously sweet smell emanates from the container, and then he takes a sip, a unique flavor dancing on his tongue.

"This must be… Coca Cola!" The man's laughter fills the air as he passes the bottle to his friends so they can savor the symbolic drink.

———————⟪✢⟫———————

About two hours have passed since the first aircraft spotted them. The planes take turns to monitor the raft, their engines rumbling as they soar in circles overhead. Every thirty minutes, the air buzzes with the sound of a new plane flying in to replace the one on guard. The planes remain unrelenting in their watch, keeping the raft in sight until the US Coast Guard arrives.

"What's taking them so long?" Carlos asks. Patience has always been his weakness.

At that precise moment, a speck flying very low in the northwestern sky catches Gerardo's attention.

"Here comes another one," he says, pointing at the distant aircraft.

"And the US Coast Guard is right behind!" Gonzalez jumps in surprise, his voice ringing out.

Sure enough, a dark dot on a padded blanket of foam is approaching at high speed, trailing behind the airplane.

"Let's roll up the sails!" Roberto's command leads the crew into action.

The men move with lightness and speed, like on the first day of their adventure. They have forgotten the grueling exhaustion of so many hours of sailing without rest as a sense of renewed energy vibrates in their bodies. Carlos and Raul rush to wrap the smaller sail, rolling it on its boom and tying it to the forestay, the rope holding the mast to the bow. From the stern, Gerardo loosens the mainsail tensor as Roberto pulls the canvas in, making the boat stop. Gerardo crawls next to Roberto and helps him raise and secure the boom to the mast.

The US Coast Guard approaches fast, the roar of its engine gradually subsiding and the foam cushion supporting it dissipating. The modern ship halts, its imposing presence contrasting with the rustic sailboat as both ships' crews are in awe of the surreal encounter. Two different worlds collide; one is a paragon of developed civilization, the other stuck in the bleakness of third-world backwardness. On the deck of the American vessel, its crew stands poised and ready to assist the exhausted rafters.

Unlike those coming by boat, people on rafts are often rescued in critical conditions. They are suffering from severe dehydration, malnourishment, burns, and other illnesses leading to loss of consciousness or death. The US Coast Guard team is well aware of this and is therefore armed with first aid kits and life jackets, ready to execute swift rescue operations.

The vast ship cautiously edges closer to the small raft, but the restless sea disrupts its progress. Despite the ship's enormous size, the waves sway the floating fortress back and forth like a weightless toy. Its crew fears that they could ram the fragile vessel in any of these swings, possibly bringing fatal consequences to its occupants.

After several unsuccessful attempts, Carlos proposes an alternative plan.

"I think it's better that we approach them."

"You're right!" his brother says, standing up and signaling the Coast Guard's crew to stop as Carlos adjusts the front oars and rows.

Esperanza moves cautiously toward its colossal neighbor while both vessels rock up and down on the restless ocean. Despite the danger, the young crew presses forward, determined to board the ship and complete their journey.

Witnessing the spectacle, the rescue personnel abandon their first aid equipment and rush to the starboard rail. Some snap pictures, while others use hand signals to direct the young sailors toward a hanging ladder being lowered from the deck. The remaining crew stand by, their eyes wide with awe and admiration as they watch the raft maneuvering in the most primitive way. Everyone feels the thrill of the moment.

As the rafters prepare to moor their vessel, Roberto instructs his mates to be ready, his voice radiating confidence.

"Unstrap your safety ropes."

Carlos keeps rowing as the others work to unburden themselves of their safety lines. But the knots, tightened by the constant dampness and strain of the journey, refuse to budge. Frustrated, they resort to the crudest of tools, an old table knife, to saw through the ropes and set themselves loose.

A few feet ahead, suspended in the air, the rope ladder skims the water's surface, swinging like a snake trying to free its tail from a captor. Its wooden steps scrape and bang against the steel hull, creating a loud, wind-rattle sound; it's music to the young rafter's ears as it chants, "Reach out and touch me." Carlos grunts as he pulls the oars with all his might before lifting them up out of harm's way.

The right corner of the bow taps the side of the ship, and Carlos grabs hold of one end of the dangling ladder. Gerardo quickly secures the other end, pulling the raft flush against the metal hull.

The young men are ready to board the ship, their hearts filled with a mix of immense joy and great nostalgia. They can't help but feel a twinge of sadness as they prepare to abandon Esperanza, the boat they built with so much effort and care.

Gerardo is the first to make his way up the swaying ladder and onto the ship, his hands gripping the wooden steps. Gonzalez takes Gerardo's position, holding the ladder as Carlos rushes to free himself from his safety rope. Once released, the young man returns to hold the ladder. Gonzalez is the second to abandon the raft, his movements slow and cautious as he climbs. With a fast arm swing, Roberto grabs the rope and pulls down the ladder, reducing its back-and-forth motion. Carlos begins his way up, Roberto's eyes fixed on his brother's back while Raul takes Carlos's place, holding one end of the ladder. The group's navigator is about to climb, but something stops him. An unexplained sensation makes him look back. He must be the last one to abandon ship.

"I can't leave yet," Roberto thinks, stepping aside and leaving the path free for Raul. "Go ahead. I'll be right behind you!"

Raul labors hard as he ascends the ladder, his body shaking in exhaustion. Holding both ropes to ease the ladder's movement, Roberto watches, his gaze locked on Raul's every step. As Raul struggles upward, he loses his footing between two steps. His body swings, suspended in the air as he clings to the ladder, hugging it against his chest. With a quick and instinctive reaction, Roberto releases one grip to free his hand and reaches out to catch his friend's right heel. Raul recovers and looks down at his friend, his eyes wide open in shock and gratitude. He stays still for a moment and takes a deep breath, regaining control over his mind before continuing forward.

With a heavy heart, the group's navigator readies himself to climb aboard the Coast Guard's vessel. His hands grip the ladder tightly as one foot rests on the first wooden step. Roberto's eyes linger on the raft, the loyal companion of their journey, filled with fond memories of the trials they overcame together. Reluctantly, he tears his gaze away and follows the others, leaving Esperanza, their heroic friend, free.

As he climbs the ladder, he can't help but take one last look at their trusty vessel, now bobbing in the sea behind him.

The five exhausted men stand on the Coast Guard's deck and are greeted with warm smiles. With crumpled hats and soaked clothes still dripping, they wave goodbye to the pilots now heading back to the mainland. Weary from their journey, the rafters gather at the starboard rail, the sun warming their faces as they look toward the southern horizon. Their homes, loved ones, and cherished memories lie many miles beyond the distant line. They stand there, lost in thought with an overwhelming sense of gratitude for their rescue and a deep longing for the home they left behind. Tears trickle down their faces as they stand motionless. The only sound is the rhythm of the waves striking the hull below. They understand the journey to reunite with their families will be long and arduous.

Adrift, Esperanza sails away from the ship, embarking on a new journey, an endless pilgrimage toward glory and history. The unspeakable nostalgia of her departure clouds the rafters' joy. In their hearts, they knew the end of their expedition would also mean the end of Esperanza, their unconditional ally.

Free from her human load, Esperanza dances on the sea's crested surface, and her mast swings to the waves' beat as a sign of farewell.

"Goodbye, friend," they whisper as tears wipe the smiles from their faces and a sense of loss fills their hearts.

It's three o'clock. Their dangerous odyssey has ended, and a new life's doors open for these daring men. About sixty-five hours have passed since they left, sixty-five hours of uncertainty, insomnia, and agony, sixty-five hours clinging to a hope named Esperanza.

In the distance, the small *Cessna Skymaster* looks like a seagull. Photo taken by Raul.

The airplane flies low in front of the small boat. Both crews greet each other. These are emotional moments. Photo taken by Raul.

Roberto and Gerardo celebrate the plane's presence. Note the exhaustion on their faces and their hats damaged by the storm surge. Photo taken by Raul.

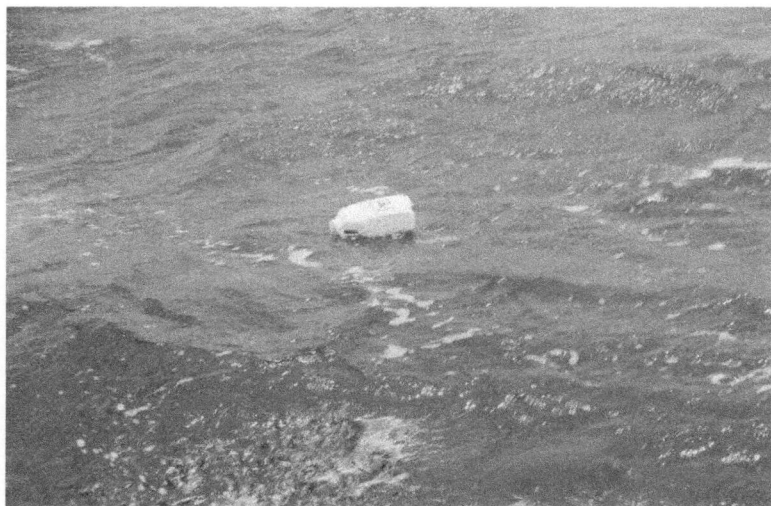

Message launched from the plane. Photo taken by Raul.

Gonzalez holds the plastic bottle thrown from the plane, while Gerardo shows the message sent inside the container, *"Welcome to the land of freedom. US Coast Guard on the way. God is with you. Brothers to the Rescue."* Photo taken by Raul.

HOPE

Hope. Right-side view (starboard). Designed by Roberto. Built by the brothers Carlos and Roberto in the attic of their house, in *El Calvario,* Havana City, Cuba.

Note: Gerardo and Raul also helped in the construction and search for materials.

POSTSCRIPT

On the afternoon of May 27, 1993, the United States Coast Guard Cutter Seahawk WSES-2 successfully retrieved five rafters. The rescue took place at approximately 34 miles southeast of Marathon Key, at the coordinates 24.9 North and 82.7 West. According to the 'Brothers to the Rescue' pilots, the rafters exhibited impressive seafaring skills. Their raft's unique characteristics and the crew's adept maneuvers showed they could have reached Miami unassisted.

Completing their patrol mission, the coast guard vessel docked in Key West around 12:30 a.m. on Friday, May 28. Immigration officials interviewed the young sailors before moving them to La Casa del Balsero, a transit home for Cuban refugees. The following morning saw the group relocating to Miami, where relatives and friends claimed their custody.

Back in their hometown in Cuba, news of their safe arrival spread like wildfire after being broadcast on Radio Martí. Overwhelmed with joy, dozens of residents from the El Calvario neighborhood rushed to the homes of Carlos and Roberto to confirm the exhilarating news. Everyone hugged and congratulated Carmen.

In a significant policy shift, the Cuban Adjustment Act underwent changes in August 1994 that dramatically impacted the fate of sea-bound escapees. No longer offering the same protections, the amendment stipulated that any rafters intercepted at sea—even within US territorial waters—would henceforth be returned to Cuban authorities. This alteration in law marked a stark departure from previous policies, raising concern and criticism among those advocating for the rights and freedom of Cuban refugees.

US Coast Guard Cutter *Seahawk WSES-2* tasked with rescuing these rafters. Retired in 1994.

Cessna Skymaster, a twin-engine civil aircraft used by 'Brothers to the Rescue.' On February 24, 1996, two of these aircraft were shot down by *MIG-29* planes in international airspace, killing all four occupants. The incident stands as a somber testament to the perils faced by those attempting to aid Cuban refugees and raises serious questions about international law and human rights. Photo courtesy of *Shoot Down* (documentary, 2007). Photographer: Claudia Raschke-Robinson.

ARMANDO ALEJANDRE   CARLOS COSTA   MARIO DE LA PEÑA   PABLO MORALES

Members of *Brothers to the Rescue* killed on February 24, 1996. Photo courtesy of EFE.

TEN YEARS LATER

To honor their harrowing journey, Carlos and Roberto constructed a meticulous replica of their original raft and christened it *Esperanza II*. Using the original blueprints sent from Cuba, the brothers painstakingly recreated the vessel, ensuring its authenticity down to the last detail. *Esperanza II* featured prominently in the award-winning documentary *Black & Blue: A Rafter's Journey*.

Produced and directed by New Jersey City-based independent filmmaker Carmen López, the 60-minute film received critical acclaim, garnering *Best Documentary*, *Best Film*, and *Audience Award* honors at film festivals in Miami and New York in 2003 and 2004. The documentary not only captures the perilous odyssey faced by rafters but also serves as a living testament to the resilience and courage that defines their pursuit of freedom.

Hope II. Photo taken during the filming of the documentary *Black & Blue: A Rafter's Journey.* From left to right, Leo Fraser (member of the film crew), Carmen López (producer and director), Roberto Morales (seated at the helm), and Carlos Morales (standing with hat in hand).

TRIBUTE TO THE CREW

To my fellow travelers: Carlos, Gerardo, Raul, and Gonzalez.

Our expedition was fraught with dangers that many can scarcely imagine, yet we persevered, united in our shared dream of freedom. Your courage, resilience, and indomitable spirits were not just my support but also my inspiration. In the darkest hours, when the seas roared and our path seemed unclear, your faith became my beacon.

Carlos R. Morales

Gerardo Pérez

Raúl Gonzalez

Jesús Gonzalez

BEYOND THE HORIZON: A NEW LIFE

Shortly after their arrival in Miami, the crew embarked on lengthy journeys toward family reunification.

A year after their departure, the two brothers were reunited with their Grandma Cuca in Miami. However, time brought a contrasting sorrow as their other grandmother, Zoila, passed away on the island. The Cuban government's stringent policies prevented them from attending her funeral, leaving an indelible mark of loss. It would be a taxing nine years before Carmen could make the emotional journey to finally reunite with her two sons on foreign soil.

Carlos waited five years before being able to travel back to the island and see his son again.

After eighteen years, Roberto returned to Cuba to visit his sister, Zady, and meet his niece. He also fulfilled his promise of returning to the beach made almost two decades before.

Both Raul and his cousin, Gonzalez, reunited with their mothers a few years after their departure.

Gerardo was reunited with his mother, Estela, but his father, Mr. Perez, stayed behind, waiting for his visa approval. He died on the island six years later. His heart could not endure the pain. His premature passing occurred three months before the US immigration service granted his traveling visa. Gerardo resolved to never go back to Cuba. "There is nothing but painful memories for me there," he says.

As time passed, Esperanza's crew gradually rebuilt their lives. They learned to move forward and discovered love in their new homeland. Their emotional scars, invisible to the naked eye, are constant reminders of the people they left behind.

Zady's visa was granted in 2015, enabling her to move to Miami with her daughter, but Carlos' son remains in Cuba. The two brothers have filed several petitions for reunification, but for unknown reasons, they have been delayed or remain unanswered.

ABOUT THE AUTHOR

Born in Havana city, Cuba in 1966, Roberto Morales emerged from humble beginnings. The second of three brothers, he was raised in a working-class household that was, above all, a haven of love and normalcy. However, tragedy struck early with the sudden death of his father when he was just 12 years old, propelling him into an accelerated journey toward maturity.

By the age of 17, Roberto's passion for sports and an intrinsic sense of duty made him the country's youngest National Orienteering Sports referee. Within just a year, he ascended to a position on the provincial commission for the sport, affirming his rising status in the field.

After fulfilling a three-year tour of mandatory military service, Roberto joined the Higher Institute of Physical Culture in Havana in 1989. Almost immediately, he distinguished himself, garnering top grades and earning the esteem of his educators and peers alike. Yet, just as he was on the cusp of completing his degree, Roberto made a shocking decision—he fled Cuba. While his departure stunned his acquaintances, it was the culmination of two years of covert and painstaking planning for Roberto and his four companions.

The crucial moment arrived on May 27, 1993. After nearly three perilous days at sea, Roberto and his group were located approximately 34 miles from Marathon Key by an aircraft from 'Brothers to the Rescue,' an organization devoted to aiding rafters in the Florida Straits. Two hours later, they were pulled to safety by the US Coast Guard.

Starting a new chapter in 1995, Roberto enrolled at Miami Dade Community College to learn English. His academic excellence was quickly acknowledged, leading him to secure several scholarships, including the *"AHEAD Balsero," "Mártires de Febrero 24,"* and *"Martha Elena Fundora"* awards. By 2000, after acing the requisite entrance exams, Roberto transitioned into a stable career as a mail carrier for the United States Postal Service.

This remarkable odyssey, from humble Cuban streets to academic accolades and a new life in the United States, encapsulates Roberto Morales; a man forged by adversity, driven by responsibility and, ultimately, redeemed through relentless pursuit of opportunity.

In 2010, Roberto and his brother Carlos co-founded Umbrellas 4 Boats, Inc. As an avid boating enthusiast, Carlos soon discovered the need for shade to protect his young children from excessive sun exposure while they played in the water. The brothers invented a base that allows a patio umbrella to be attached to the back of a boat. Umbrellas 4 Boats has been very well received by users of the product.

Roberto (left) and Carlos (right) promoting *Umbrellas 4 Boats* (umbrellas4boats.com).

Would you recommend this book?

Please send us your comments and share. Your written review is highly appreciated, and it will help other readers to find us.

Available formats:

❖ Print
❖ E-book
❖ Audiobook

https://www.facebook.com/Esperanza.libro